Dr Jekyll & Mr Hyde

A new stage version by Glyn Maxwell
Based on the novel by Robert Louis Stevenson

The Strange Case of Dr Jekyll & Mr Hyde was first performed at Storyhouse, Chester, on 5 October 2019 with the following cast and creative team:

Cast

Natasha Bain **Lady Gabriel**

Matthew Flynn **Mr Hyde**

Edward Harrison **Dr Jekyll**

Rosa Hesmondhalgh **Rose**

Creative Team

Psyche Stott **Director**

Katie Lias **Designer**

Neill Brinkworth **Lighting Designer**

Adrienne Quartly **Sound Designer and Composer**

Sarah Richardson **Assistant Director**

Paul Bayes Kitcher **Choreographer**

Kay Magson **Casting Director**

Paul Benzing **Fight Director**

CAST

NATASHA BAIN **LADY GABRIEL**

For Storyhouse: Aunt Em and The Good Witch of the North in
The Wizard of Oz, Tituba in *The Crucible* and Mrs Nordstrom in
A Little Night Music, all 2018.

Natasha's recent credits include: Islander in *The Third Day* (HBO/
Sky Prod) The Dodo in *Trace New Diorama*, Francisca in *Wonder
Girl First* Bites (Festival Oval House); Mrs Nordstrom in *A Little
Night Music* (Storyhouse); Tituba in *The* Crucible (Storyhouse);
Aunty Em and The Good Witch in *The Wizard of Oz* (Storyhouse).

Other stage work includes: Isabel & Northumberland in *Richard
II* (The Arcola) *In The Blood* (Finborough); *The Wedding Dance*
(Bolton Octagon); *The Royal Hunt of The Sun* (National Theatre);
The Lion & The Jewel (Barbican Theatre); *The Gondoliers/The
Water Babies* (Chichester); *The Lion* King (Lyceum) *Merry Wives
of Windsor & Twelfth Night* (Regents Park Open Air); *The Amen
Corner* (Bristol Old Vic); *The Red Balloon* (Birmingham Rep/
National Theatre) and *The Threepenny Opera* (Donmar).

Television credits include: *Doctors*, *Rough Treatment*, *The Bill*,
Casualty, *In Your Dreams*, *Waiting for God*, *Grange Hill*.

Film credits include *Life in Orbit*, *Fluid*, *Greys Inbetween*,
Offending Angels, *Harvest Festival* and the BAFTA winning *Zinky
Boys Go Underground*.

MATTHEW FLYNN **MR HYDE**

For Storyhouse, John Proctor in *The Crucible*, 2018.

Theatre credits include: *Agnes Colander* (Ustinov Bath); *Child
of Science* (Bush); *City stories* (59e59 Theatre New York); *I am
a Walrus* (Young Vic); *WarHorse* (National Theatre/West End);
Children of the Sun (National Theatre); *Mare Rider* (Arcola); *55
Days and Wild Honey* (Hampstead; *Henry Vth and Troilus and
Cressida* (Globe Theatre); *A Streetcar Named Desire* (Liverpool
Playhouse); *The Two Gentlemen of Verona* (Northampton);
Macbeth and *The Mayor of Zalamea* (Liverpool Everyman);
As You Like It, *Macbeth and How Many Miles to Basra?* (West
Yorkshire Playhouse); *1984* and *Julius Caesar* (Manchester Royal

Exchange); *The Gentlemen's Tea Drinking Society* (Belfast); *Hangover Square* (Finborough); *Our Friends in the North* (Northern Stage); *Romeo and Juliet* (Derby); *The Winters' Tale*, *A Midsummer Nights Dream*, *Rose Rage*, *Twelfth Night*, *Comedy of Errors*, *Henry Vth* (Propeller/West End/New York and World Tours); *The Prince of Homburg*, *Romeo and Juliet and Julius Caesar* (RSC); *Hamlet* (Bristol Old Vic); *Meat* (Plymouth); *A View from the Bridge* (Touring Consortium); *Othello* (Watermill); *An Ideal Husband* (West End).

Television credits include: *Innocent* (ITV) *Lawful Killing* (BBC); *Doctors* (BBC); *Coronation St* (ITV); *Lucan* (ITV); *Holby City* (BBC); *Midsomer Murders* (BBC); *Foyles War* (ITV); *The Passion* (HBO,BBC); *After Thomas* (ITV); *The Quatermass Experiment* (BBC); *The King Must Die* (CH4); *A Class Act* (ITV); *Tell me no Lies* (CH4); *Trial and Retribution* (ITV); *The Final Passage* (CH4).

Film credits include: *Pride*, *Broken Lines*, *Franklyn*, *Sahara*.

EDWARD HARRISON **DR JEKYLL**

For Grosvenor Park Open Air Theatre: Cyrano in *Cyrano de Bergerac*, *A Midsummer Night's Dream* and *Othello*, all 2013

Theatre credits include: *Skellig* (Nottingham Playhouse); *Shakespeare in Love* (Theatre Royal Bath & Eleanor Lloyd Productions UK Tour); *Holes* (Nottingham Playhouse); *Baskerville* (Liverpool Playhouse) *Constellations* (Singapore Repertory Theatre); *All my Sons* (Rose Theatre, Kingston); *Wolf Hall*, *Bring Up the Bodies* (Royal Shakespeare Company, Winter Garden Theatre, Broadway); *Henry V* (Michael Grandage Company, Noel Coward Theatre, West End); *Macbeth* (Kenneth Branagh, Armory, New York); *Tomcat* (Southwark Playhouse);*Taming of the Shrew*, *Cyrano de Bergerac* (US Tour); *The Rivals* (Theatre Royal Haymarket, West End and UK Tour); *Henry IV Part One and Part Two* (Peter Hall Company, Theatre Royal Bath); *Cyrano de Bergerac*, *A Midsummer Night's Dream*, *Othello*, (Grosvenor Park Open Air Theatre); *Joking Apart*, *Time and the Conway's* (Nottingham Playhouse); *Noises Off!*, *Norman Conquests and Accidental Death of An Anarchist* (Torch Theatre) and *Dangerous Liaisons*, *She Stoops to Conquer* (Mappa Mundi, UK Tour).

Television credits include: Eastenders (BBC); *Genius* (Fox21/NatGeo); *Doctor Who* (BBC); *Doctors* (BBC)

Film credits include: ***Brandoing*** (Virgin Short Finalist); ***The Present***, ***Dante***, ***Breathing Room***, ***Oska Bayte***.

Radio credits include: ***Dorian Gray***, ***Doctor Who: Nightshade and Vienna: Retribution*** (Big Finish); ***Darkwater Bride***, ***Unseen Academicals***, ***A Doll's House***, ***Enemy of the People***, ***Treasure Island and Just One Damned Thing After Another*** (Audible).

ROSA HESMONDHALGH **ROSE**

Rosa graduated from LAMDA in 2017.

Theatre credits include: Belle in ***A Christmas Carol*** (Hull Truck); Mary Oliver in ***Trial By Laughter*** (Watermill and UK Tour) and Rachel in ***Just A Woman*** (BBC Radio 4). Rosa has also just returned from Edinburgh where she wrote and performed in her critically acclaimed one woman show, ***Madame Ovary***. It will tour in 2020.

CREATIVE TEAM

GLYN MAXWELL **WRITER**

Glyn is an award-winning poet, playwright, novelist and librettist. Born and raised in Hertfordshire, his roots lie in the Wirral and North Wales.

For Grosvenor Park Open Air Theatre and Storyhouse: *The Secret Seven* (2017); *Alice in Wonderland* (2017); *The Beggar's Opera* (2017); *Wind In The Willows* (2015); *Cyrano de Bergerac* (2013); *Masters Are You Mad?* (2012); *Merlin and the Woods of Time* (2011).

Poetry credits includes: *Pluto* (2013); *One Thousand Nights and Counting* (2011); *Hide Now* (2008); *The Sugar Mile* (2005); *The Nerve* (2003); *Time's Fool* (2000).

Theatre credits include: *Babette's Feast* (Print Room, 2017); *Cyrano De Bergerac* (Southwark Playhouse, 2016); *The Gambler* (Wild Project, NYC, 2016); *After Troy* (Shaw, Oxford Playhouse, 2011); *Liberty* (Shakespeare's Globe, UK Tour, 2008); *The Only Girl in The World* (Arcola, 2008); *The Lifeblood* (Edinburgh Fringe, Riverside, 2005); *The Forever Waltz* (Workshop Theatre NYC, Edinburgh Fringe, 2004); *The Last Valentine* (Almeida, 2000); *Broken Journey* (Hen & Chickens, 1999).

Opera libretti credits include: *The Magic Flute* (Soho Theatre, UK Tour, 2017); *Nothing* (Glyndebourne 2016, composer David Bruce); *The Firework Maker's Daughter* (Royal Opera House, New Victory NYC, UK Tour, 2013, composer David Bruce); *Seven Angels* (Royal Opera House, UK Tour, 2011, composer Luke Bedford); *The Lion's Face* (Royal Opera House, Opera North, UK Tour, 2010, composer Elena Langer).

Criticism credits include: *On Poetry* (2012).

Fiction credits inclide: *Drinks With Dead Poets* (2016).

Film credits: *The Beast in the Jungle* (KeyFilm/Amour Fou, 2017).

DIRECTOR **PSYCHE STOTT**

Psyche is a freelance Theatre Director. Her work has taken her to Rome, Australia, Europe and throughout the UK, enabling her to work in Regional Theatre, West End as well as on National and International Tours.

Forth coming productions include: *The Secret Life of Humans* by David Byrne for The English Theatre Frankfurt 40th Anniversary Season in 2020.

In 2006 she won the Channel 4 Regional Directors Award (now the Regional Theatre Young Director Award) enabling her to work as Director in Residence, mentored by Erica Whyman at Northern Stage alongside a wealth of international visiting artists including Robert Lepage and his company Ex-Machina, who spent six weeks in residence with Northern stage developing Lypsynch. Psyche continued with Northern Stage as Associate Director for their UK tour of Our Friends in the North. Training includes the National Theatre Studio.

Psyche regularly supports the work of emerging artists in her capacity as a selector for NSDF www.nsdf.org.uk and as, Connections Director, for the National Theatre. She is also a regular guest Director for the Royal Academy of Dramatic Art and is currently on the audition panel for RADA.

Previous productions for RADA include: *Suddenly Last Summer / Something Unspoken*; *Kindertransport*; *The Five Wives of Maurice Pinder*; *Women of Twilight*.

Directing highlights include: *The Children* (The English Theatre Frankfurt); *Lucy Kirkwoods* (NSFW, Platform Theatre London); *The 20th anniversary production of David Farrs*, *Elton John's Glasses* (Watford Palace Theatre); *The Fighting Bradfords* (new commision, Gala Theatre, Durham); *Blue Remembered Hills* (Northern Stage & UK Tour); *Skylight* (Teatro Dell'Orologio, Rome); *Come Back to the Five* and *Dime Jimmy Dean Jimmy Dean* (Old Joint Stock Theatre); the Australian Premiere of the Award winning British hit comedy *Calendar Girls* (for Gordon Frost Organisation, Lyric Theatre, QPAC Brisbane, Theatre Royal Sydney and Comedy Theatre Melbourne); *Calendar Girls*

(Jan – Apr 2010 Chichester Festival Theatre and New UK Tour); **Pub Quiz** (New Writing North and Northeast Theatre Consortium Regional Tour).

Directing for BBC Radio includes: Brian Friel's **Hedda Gabler** (produced by Sparklab for BBC Radio 4)

Associate Director credits include: **Wind in the Willows** (Stiles and Drewe musical, West End & UK Tour); **Impossible** (Jamie Hendry Productions, Singapore); **The Illusionists Live** (UK, Dubai & European Tour & ITV XMAS SPECIAL 2013); **Calendar Girls** (Original UK Tour & West End); **Our Friends in the North** (Northern Stage & UK Tour).

You can find out more at her website www.psychestott.co.uk

KATIE LIAS **DESIGNER**

Katie trained at Rada and was Resident Design Assistant at the RSC. She has assisted on numerous productions in the West End and at the National Theatre. She is an Associate Artist at The Watermill.

Credits include: **The Prince and the Pauper, Macbeth, A Midsummer Night's Dream**, **Twelfth Night, Romeo and Juliet, Journey's End** (Watermill); **Eclipse, Cinderella** and **Dick Whittington and His Cat** (Lyric Hammersmith); **Valhalla, Coalition, Word: Play 3** (503); **The Lone Pine Club** (Pentabus**)**; **Polka40, Grandad, Me and Teddy Too, Alice in Wonderland, Shake Rattle and Roll, My Brother My Sister and Me** (Polka); **Nanny McPhee** (costumes, London Children's Ballet); **Address Unknown** (Soho); **The Welsh Boy, Deadkindssongs** (costumes, Ustinov Studio, Bath); **The Tempest, Shakespeare In A Suitcase** (RSC Tour); **Treasure Island, Love and Information, The Addams Family, Antigone, Song Cycles** and **Table** (Arts Ed); **In The Summer House, Penthesilea** and **Man Equals Man** (RADA); **Tinderbox** (Tooting Arts Club).

NEILL BRINKWORTH **LIGHTING DESIGNER**

Recent credits include: *The Firm* (Hampstead Theatre); *The Dark* (Fuel Theatre); *Dark Sublime* (Trafalgar Studios); *Coat* (Roundhouse); *[BLANK]* (NT Connections, Dorfmann Theatre); *Billy The Kid* (NYMT, Leicester Curve); *Hansel und Gretl*, revival (San Francisco Opera); *The Meeting* (Hampstead Theatre); *In the Night Garden Live* (Minor Entertainment); *Lohengrin, revival* (National Opera of Greece, Polish National Opera); *Tamburlaine* (Yellow Earth); *Mozart vs Machine* (Mahogany Opera); *Children of Killers* (NT Connections, Olivier Theatre); *Dido & Aeneas* (English Touring Opera); *As Is* (Trafalgar Studios); *Sweat Factory* (YMT, Sadler's Wells); *Dessa Rose* (Trafalgar Studios); *Café Chaos; A Square of Sky* (The Kosh); *The Seagull* (Arcola); *Strauss Gala* (Raymond Gubbay); *Bridgetower* (City of London Festival/ ETO); *Vincent River* (Old Vic productions); *Antigone*; *Lysistrata*; *Prometheus*; *The Frogs*; *Agamemnon* (all Cambridge Arts Theatre).

As Associate Lighting Designer: *Everybody's Talking About Jamie* (Apollo, West End); *Ludd & Isis* (ROH); *Maria Stuarda* (Opera North); *Symbionts* (Wayne McGregor, Estonia National Ballet); *O* (Michael Clarke Dance Company).

ADRIENNE QUARTLY **SOUND DESIGNER AND COMPOSER**

Adrienne is a Sound designer/Composer for Theatre. Her work has been presented all over the world.

Recent shows include: *The Girl Who Fell (*Trafalgar Studios); *Citysong* (Abbey Theatre, Dublin/Soho); *Queen Margaret,* (Royal Exchange, Manchester); *The Paper Man* (Improbable Theatre); *Black Men Walking* (Royal Court Theatre); *Kindertransport*, *The Crucible* (Les Théâtres de la Ville de Luxembourg); *Get Happy* (Beijing Comedy Festival); *Opening Skinners Box*, (Lincoln Centre Festival, New York); *A Tale of Two Cities*, (Royal and Derngate, Northampton); *Bad Jews*, Theatre Royal, Haymarket, *I am Thoma*s (Told By an Idiot, NTS); *Splendour*, (Donmar Warehouse); *The Ghost Train* (Told by an Idiot); *Inside Wagner's Head*, (Royal Opera House); *Frauline Julie(* Schaubühne, Berlin/ Barbican); *Rings of Saturn*, (Halle Kalk, Cologne); *Thomas Hobbes, Mary Schindler*, RSC.

Adrienne was part of the team behind the Olivier nominated production of **Cuttin' It** (Young Vic Theatre); best new play nomination for UK theatre awards **Black Men Walking** (Eclipse); and best production at Manchester Theatre Awards **Rose** (Home).

Audiodrama credits include: **Hefted** by David Lane (Beaford Arts); Finalist for The Audible Audio drama Competition with Hannah Price.

www.adriennequartly.com

SARAH RICHARDSON **ASSISTANT DIRECTOR**

For Grosvenor Park Open Air Theatre: **The Borrowers,** 2019.

Sarah is a freelance director and Co-Director of Filament Projects.

Directing credits include: **A Muddle in Messina**, a re-telling of Shakespeare's **Much Ado About Nothing** for young audiences created in partnership with Northern Broadsides and **To Stop Her Mouth**, an audio installation exploring the 1826 abduction of Ellen Turner, a 15 year old heiress, commissioned by Waterside Arts and Trust New Art.

Assisting credits include: **Little Voice**, dir. Zoë Waterman, Theatre By The Lake and **The Borrowers**, dir. Robert Shaw Cameron, Storyhouse.

Prior to directing Sarah was a member of the New Vic Education team at the New Vic Theatre creating projects with children, schools and libraries and developing Tale Trail, an annual immersive production for 3-5 year olds, now in its eleventh year.

Sarah is a current recipient of an Arts Council England Developing Your Creative Practice grant.

PAUL BAYES KITCHER **CHOREOGRAPHER**

Paul trained at the Royal Ballet School and at Rambert.

Performer credits include: Various principal roles for Scottish Ballet including **Don Q Pas de Deux**, Peter Darrell's **Cheri** and Balanchine's **Scotch Symphony**. Kirov Ballet Oleg Vinagradov, **La Vivandier**. Birmingham Royal Ballet, First Artist and Soloist roles included Paul Taylor's **Airs**, BlueBird Pas de deux, Benno in

Swan Lake and The Principal in Balanchine's *Symphony in Three Movements*. Paul has worked with choreographers Michael Corder, David Bintley, Sir Peter Wright and Sir Kenneth Macmillan.

Workshops and outreach credits include projects for The Royal Ballet School and Birmingham Royal Ballet. He taught at Carlos Acosta, Random Dance Company and Trocadero's de Monte Carlo for Manchester International Festival.

In 2009 Paul began teaching within Rehabilitation settings alongside developing his artistic practice which led to him to form Fallen Angels Dance Theatre who are now company in residence at Storyhouse. The company's highlights have been to perform at The Royal Opera House Clore Studio, Russell Brand's book Launch *Revolution* and at a Parliamentary Seminar at the Embassy of Brazil. Paul was also invited to speak with Mitch Winehouse on a panel discussion at the House of Commons.

Today he develops and directs professional work, delivers participatory projects within criminal justice, addiction/recovery rehabilitation and community settings, and is an inspirational public speaker. In the last year Paul has delivered two TEDx talks, BBC3 devoted an *Amazing Humans* short film to his journey to supporting people in recovery from addiction through dance theatre, and his return to Birmingham Royal Ballet, as well as meeting Her Majesty the Queen with HRH Duchess of Sussex at Storyhouse.

KAY MAGSON **CASTING DIRECTOR**

Kay Magson has cast all ten seasons of Grosvenor Park Open Air Theatre, as well as all of Storyhouse's home-produced shows.

Theatre credits include*: The Solid Gold Cadillac* (Garrick); *Dangerous Corner* (West Yorkshire Playhouse/ West End); *Round the Horne... Revisited, Dracula* (National tours); *Singin' in the Rain* (West Yorkshire Playhouse, NT/ National tour); *spects of Love, All The Fun of the Fair and The Witches of Eastwick* (National Tours); *Kes* (Liverpool and National Tour); *Great Expectations* (ETT/ Watford and National tour); *Sweeney Todd* (Royal Festival Hall) and national tours of *Beautiful Thing, James & The Giant Peach, Horrible Histories* and many more.

Kay was resident at the West Yorkshire Playhouse for 17 years where she cast many shows including the McKellen Ensemble Season, the Patrick Stewart PriestleySeason and others, and casts regularly for Liverpool Everyman and Playhouse, Leicester Curve, Derby Theatre, Sherman Cardiff and the West Yorkshire Playhouse where she is Associate Artist (Casting). Kay is a member of the Casting Director's Guild of Great Britain (CDG).

PAUL BENZING **FIGHT DIRECTOR**

Paul is on the Equity Fight Directors Register and a member of The BADC.

Fight directing credits include: *Journeys End* (The Comedy Theatre); *Hamlet* (Young Vic and The Nuffield Theatre Southampton); *National Anthem* (Old Vic); *Edward Bond's Lear, Who's Afraid of Virginia Woolf?* (The Crucible Theatre Sheffield); *Manchester Passion* (BBC); *Clockwork Orange, Son Of Man, Our Friends In The North, Close The Coalhouse Door, Get Carter* (Northern Stage); *The Country Wife, The Sea, Marguerite* (The Theatre Royal Haymarket); *Black Comedy, Moonlight & Magnolias, Of Mice & Men, House and Garden* (The Watermill Newbury); *Troilus and Cressida* (Cheek By Jowl); *West Side Story* (Wandsworth Prison); *Dreams of Violence, Flight Path* (Out Of Joint); *Othello* (The Ludlow Festival); *Zadia* (Classic Opera Co.); *What The Butler Saw, Slaves of Solitude* (Hampstead Theatre); *Oleanna* (The Lakeside Nottingham); *Comedy Of Errors, Into The Woods, Turn of the Screw* (Regents Park); *Mother Courage, Revengers Tragedy, Nation, Emperor & Galilean, Antigone, Downstate, Peter Gynt* (National Theatre); *Ross, Young Chekhovs, Sweet Bird of Youth* (Chichester Festival Theatre); *Making Noise Quietly* (Donmar Warehouse); *Sweeney Todd* (The Adelphi); *West Side Story* (The Sage Gateshead); *Don Giovanni* (Glyndebourne); *Seven Acts of Mercy* (RSC); *Baskerville* (Liverpool Playhouse); *Crazy for You* (tour); *The Children* (The English Theater Frankfurt); *War Horse* (UK tour and West End).

STORYHOUSE

WELCOME TO STORYHOUSE!

Storyhouse is a multi-award winning theatre, library, cinema, restaurant and community hub. It welcomes over a million visits a year.

The pioneering new library within Storyhouse, where members of the community work alongside city librarians, has the longest opening hours of any UK public library and is open every day until 11pm. Storyhouse offers over 2,500 storytelling, arts, crafts and music activities each year.

The organisation houses a nationally-acclaimed theatre company with home-produced stage shows each year. Storyhouse also founded and runs the country's most successful regional open-air theatre company, Grosvenor Park Open Air Theatre, in the city's main park, and an open-air cinema, Moonlight Flicks. Storyhouse's independent cinema screens a handpicked programme of world, independent and mainstream film.

Storyhouse produces a raft of creative festivals including, Chester Literature Festival, Chester Music Festival, Storyhouse Women, Storyhouse Parent, Storyhouse Languages, Love Later Life, The Great Get Together and Kaleidoscope.

Find out more at **storyhouse.com**

DR JEKYLL & MR HYDE

A new stage version by Glyn Maxwell

Based on the novel by Robert Louis Stevenson

OBERON BOOKS
LONDON

WWW.OBERONBOOKS.COM

First published in 2019 by Oberon Books Ltd
521 Caledonian Road, London N7 9RH
Tel: +44 (0) 20 7607 3637 / Fax: +44 (0) 20 7607 3629
e-mail: info@oberonbooks.com
www.oberonbooks.com

A catalogue record for this book is available from the British Library.

PB ISBN: 9781786829511
E ISBN: 9781786829528

Cover design by AKA

Visit www.oberonbooks.com to read more about all our books and to buy them. You will
also find features, author interviews and news of any author events, and you can sign up for
e-newsletters and be the first to hear about our new releases.

Printed on FSC® accredited paper

10 9 8 7 6 5 4 3 2 1

Characters

DR JEKYLL
MR HYDE
LADY GABRIEL UTTERSON
MISS ROSE PALFREY

Other parts played by the company

*'For about him till the very end were still
those he had studied, the fauna of the night,
and shades that still waited to enter
the bright circle of his recognition
turned elsewhere...'*

W. H. Auden, *In Memory of Sigmund Freud*

1

Darkness

FIGURES between darkness and light

Light. Something weeping

JEKYLL waking, reaching for his notebook

JEKYLL: Coming home... from some place – as if end of
the world – about three o'clock, black winter morning –
way lies through a part of town – nothing to be seen but
lamps... street after street, all the folks asleep – empty as a
church... do not remember walking here, or why I came,
or what I wait for...

A GIRL, loitering

JEKYLL: See a figure – girl – matchgirl just standing,
shivering, no one came to buy her matches...

A FIGURE comes from nowhere

JEKYLL: Then suddenly a man, stumping eastward at a
good walk – towards where the girl is standing, then –
horrible part of the thing – what *he* sees is what *I* see – the
matchgirl growing in my sight, the ground bouncing along
before me, over cobblestones I go, like my eyes were the
stranger's eyes, little white face does not believe I would,
draining of blood for I cannot stop, I *will* not stop, I do
not stop –

*The FIGURE cannons into her, knocks her down, tramples her, she
screams*

JEKYLL: It wasn't me, I saw it, it wasn't a man at all, to leave
a child screaming on the ground, it was like some damned
Juggernaut! Not a man – not I, not I... Then it was over,

both were gone, I saw nothing, only the empty street, the chains of lamps, I heard only – weeping, like a lost soul, and I woke with that on my heart, as if –as if I myself were the creature weeping… Lady, oh lady, help me… These dreams are overpowering, it's the compound brings them on,

He notices something

JEKYLL: And – there are – matches in my clothes…

ROSE prepares

ROSE: Rose-scented paper, so she knows it's me…

GABRIEL: George, my dear brother, how is life in Devon? I imagine you enjoy all the peace and serenity I am in want of here in London,

ROSE: And the pen with the violet ink, so she knows I mean it!

GABRIEL: I write with some urgency, in response to your request regarding your daughter: this is not a fit place and these are not fit times for a sweet soul like little Rosemary, I would exhort you for her own sake – please do not let her write to me –

ROSE: My dearest Auntie Gabriel, how are you on this fine day? 'Tis a fine sunny day in Devonshire, are there blizzards over London?

GABRIEL: As you well know I would find a direct approach from that spirited child not so easy to resist,

ROSE: This letter comes from Rosemary Palfrey, your favourite niece. My father says you were always quite the one for puzzlements and riddles, so I've made a riddle just for you:

GABRIEL: I can only disappoint the girl, so do please discourage her from any personal approach,

ROSE: When you last saw me, Auntie, I was half the height I am now and thirty-three percent in years, in five years you'll be twice my age,

GABRIEL: I am sure she's not yet eighteen,

ROSE: Wrong! Next! I am writing from my undiscovered planet so *very* far from the light of London that it appears as nothing but a distant star in my eye –

GABRIEL: Please, George, I exhort you,

ROSE: And the wise men of the parish, they think this errant twinkling can be removed by the use of damp cloths,

GABRIEL: I am sure that when the time comes, perhaps when Rose is married and of shall we say a more settled disposition,

ROSE: And my best friend Jenny Gleaner says I'll never leave the village,

GABRIEL: Moreover I am very busy this season with my charity work especially, she would be left to shift for herself, and as a young child she was ever bored and restless,

ROSE: My train arrives at the station of Waterloo at 4.19 precisely – will I be in time for the Battle? I doubt it, I have never arrived precisely *anywhere!*

GABRIEL: There is really no great space for her in my house –

ROSE: But I did! At 4.19 – oh my this house is a palace! And you live here, look at that window, all the different shades of glass!

3

GABRIEL: I do, Rosie, but then, over the years I've acquired many –

ROSE: Is this where you do your, father says you do experiments,

GABRIEL: George's mind is lingering years ago, why don't you get some rest,

ROSE: He said you'd understand me, do you think so? I do hope so, for *I* don't understand me and he most certainly don't!

GABRIEL: *Doesn't,*

ROSE: *Doesn't,* what's this, what does it measure,

GABRIEL: It's an ornament, it's nothing, now what *I* don't understand is, why did the fellows I sent to meet you arrive here with all your packages and cases and no sign of you at all?

ROSE: Why? Easy, I went walking in London Town, I told them to go ahead without me.

GABRIEL: *Why on earth would you do that*? You have never been here!

ROSE: Because I have never been here! I have just now voyaged to the realm of wonders! and she wants me to sit in a box pulled by a horse and look through a porthole at houses going by, ooh a building, another building, another building, very interesting,

GABRIEL: Oh good heavens above,

ROSE: I strolled down The Regent's Street, but I didn't meet The Regent,

GABRIEL: Small mercy you took the safest course!

ROSE: Yes no I didn't meet The Regent so I sauntered off
along a narrow lane to do my own exploring…

GABRIEL: *Please* tell me that's not true, there have been
murders, mayhem, mobs on the street,

ROSE: A few steps and the whole world altered, it was
noisier and darker, and everyone looked smaller, I felt
like Gulliver which reminds me, I must write up all my
findings in my book of wonders,

GABRIEL: Rose in heaven's name you must stay on The
Regent's Street!

ROSE: But I would not, and I did not, dear Jenny, and I shall
not, and it's three days since she said to, I am Rosemary of
London Town, in the care of Lady Utterson, and I come
and go as I please!

She goes. GABRIEL has something hidden in a drawer

JEKYLL: My old friend as I yet call you, my lost associate
in these explorations, we ever reflected deeply on the
duplicities at the heart of life. Our combined studies shed
a strong light on this consciousness, that there exists a
perennial war between conflicting elements within us.
Since your untimely departure from our enterprise, I
continued on the course we laid down as a theoretical
possibility. And with every passing day I have drawn
steadily nearer to its chemical essence – that the human
soul is not truly one, *but truly two.* Yet I know only
one soul on earth who ever understood the physical
implications of this theory. That person is yourself.

She crumples it as ROSE comes

ROSE: Aunt Gabriel, has that paper upset you?

GABRIEL: It's nothing, it's – business, an inventory of –
nothing,

ROSE: It's something now, it's a white rose in my honour!

GABRIEL: You will – *dance* so, won't you Rose,

JEKYLL: If each, I told myself, could but be housed in separate identities, life would be relieved of all that was unbearable,

ROSE: But my white rose has troubled you!

GABRIEL: I tell you, it's nothing, would you like me to tear it up before your eyes to prove it?

ROSE: I don't think that would prove it,

JEKYLL: The Unjust might go his way, delivered from his upright twin, the Just could walk steadfastly, no longer exposed to disgrace by the hands of this extraneous evil,

GABRIEL: There, pocketed, gone.

ROSE: Never even existed!

GABRIEL: A lady in my position is rather besieged by appeals for funding for the most eccentric and in some cases appalling projects,

ROSE: Was it an inventory of appalling things?

GABRIEL: We have moved on from the letter, Rose, now I was under the impression you were going to take my carriage to the talk at the Society this morning?

ROSE: I was, I did, that happened, it was a brilliant lecture on The Astrology of the Soul, whereupon a lady in a mustard waistcoat asked me to a séance,

GABRIEL: Come straight back with the boy, no dawdling, no adventures!

ROSE: But that was in the future – oh look, Aunt Gabriel,

GABRIEL: What?

A letter coming through the door

JEKYLL: I have begun to perceive more deeply than has ever yet been stated, a trembling immateriality, a mist-like transience, of this seemingly solid body in which we walk attired...

ROSE: Another thing that's nothing is coming through the door, you can grow another rose, make it disappear like magic. I have a séance to attend!

GABRIEL: What?

ROSE: Nothing!

ROSE goes, GABRIEL alone, JEKYLL only a voice from darkness

JEKYLL: Certain agents I found to have the power to shake and pluck back that fleshly vestment – even as the wind might toss the curtains of a pavilion...

GABRIEL: Do not write to me, do not think of me,

JEKYLL: To compound a drug by which these powers should be dethroned from their supremacy...

GABRIEL: No, no, I did not read these words,

JEKYLL: A second form substituted, none the less natural to me because they were the expression, and bore the stamp, of lower elements in my soul...

GABRIEL: Stop this, Henry, stop this it was folly to think it, it is lunacy to attempt it,

JEKYLL: I have hesitated long, I know that I risk death, for I have now no helpmeet to assist me in the exact proportions for the compound,

GABRIEL: I am no man's helpmeet, sir –

JEKYLL: I prepared my tincture, and late one night I blended the elements –

GABRIEL: I will not assist you in this sorcery –

JEKYLL: Watched them boil and smoke together in the glass, and when the ebullition had subsided –

Seeing another letter GABRIEL opens the door. HYDE

GABRIEL: Why do you bring these letters, sir. They have not been answered and shall not be. I say why do you bring these letters?

HYDE stares at her

GABRIEL: Sir, I ask again –

HYDE: You – have not been answered and shall not be.

GABRIEL: I *beg* your pardon?

HYDE: It is – a new day.

GABRIEL: May I ask who you are, precisely?

HYDE: I have my coat and boots.

GABRIEL: That's not what I asked you, fellow,

HYDE: You must know I come from him.

HYDE goes past her into the room

GABRIEL: Did I invite you into the house?

HYDE: You know him, you are his friend.

GABRIEL: I see, so I am to indulge his servants as I indulged his madness, no, I am not his friend.

HYDE: I am not either. Nor his servant.

GABRIEL: What?

HYDE: This is your house. Here I am in your house.

HYDE sits

GABRIEL: Did I invite you to take a seat.

HYDE: No.

GABRIEL: I – . State your business and be gone.

HYDE: You are Lady Gabriel.

GABRIEL: Not your business, but proceed.

HYDE: This is your house I am in.

GABRIEL: This is my house I would like you to be out of.

HYDE: He is a friend in need.

GABRIEL: I have said he is not my friend.

HYDE: It is otherwise.

GABRIEL: I beg – what?

HYDE: He thinks you are his friend.

GABRIEL: Well. I see. For his former friendship I shall hear you for one minute. What is his situation.

HYDE: I said. He is in need.

GABRIEL: Need of what? What is the gentleman in need of?

HYDE: Help. He is ill. He cannot leave the house. He cannot eat. He is wild.

GABRIEL: Dismal tidings, but after so long scarcely my concern.

HYDE: *She knows, she knows!* I hear him cry.

GABRIEL: She knows, *who* knows?

HYDE: The lady.

GABRIEL: She knows *what*.

HYDE: You ask me that but it's you who knows.

GABRIEL: I know nothing. I do not wish to work alongside him, I have long ago repudiated his work, the matter is closed, be gone. – Be gone, I have said.

HYDE: I have heard you.

GABRIEL: But you sit there.

HYDE: You are his only hope.

GABRIEL: Good God I am *no one's* only hope, I demand you leave now,

HYDE: This letter is his last chance.

GABRIEL: Well that's his view not mine.

HYDE: My view's the same as his.

GABRIEL: I care not what your view is.

HYDE: You are the last chance.

GABRIEL: Who are you? What are you to him?

HYDE: I am the bearer.

HYDE holds out the letter, GABRIEL takes it.

GABRIEL: (Blessed angels….) All right. You are – the bearer. You say this is a last chance. I shall take this last chance. For the sake of days gone by. Wait outside the door.

HYDE: I beg your pardon.

GABRIEL: *Please* wait outside the door.

HYDE: What.

GABRIEL: Wait outside the door or I shall rip his last chance into snowdrops.

HYDE goes slowly to the threshold, GABRIEL scans the letter carelessly

JEKYLL: Dear lady, I beg you to listen, if not to an old friend, then to a soul in torment – I have had the most vivid and terrible dream, which I can only attribute to the workings of the compound, or what I might truthfully call *our* compound…

GABRIEL *(To HYDE.)*: This will be brief, sir, I shan't finish his letter.

JEKYLL: It was at the end of the world, about three o'clock of a black winter's morning, and my way lay through a part of town where there was literally nothing to be seen but lamps…

HYDE: I shall tell him you did read it.

GABRIEL: Tell him what you please.

JEKYLL: Suddenly a man was stumping eastward at a good walk towards where the girl was standing. Then came the horrible part of the thing…

GABRIEL: I – cannot help him –

But nor can she stop reading.

JEKYLL: Then it was over, both were gone, I saw nothing, only the empty street, the chains of lamps. I heard only weeping, like a lost soul, and I awoke with that on my heart, as if I myself were the creature weeping.

GABRIEL: He tells me his dream, why so could any man or beast, and it would mean about as much to me as – *[Something at the end of the letter.]* –

JEKYLL: In the cold light of morning I found matches in my clothes.

GABRIEL crumples the letter up, and means to give it back to HYDE, but ROSE returns, and HYDE backs away into the room

ROSE: I forgot my book of wonders, auntie! I wandered such winding streets as I had never imagined, saw faces that were boiled down into stories and I reached for a blessed blank page and oh I *had* no blank page and nowhere to – oh. Where'd *you* spring from? Good afternoon.

GABRIEL: This man is leaving, Rose, it's of no importance.

ROSE: Is it you who brings the letters? She makes white roses out of them, don't you Aunt Gabriel, look she's done it again.

GABRIEL: I've no message to return to him, sir. He is delirious, he needs another doctor, all his friends are doctors, Dr Lanyon, Dr Fry, so please,

HYDE *(To ROSE.)*: What's in your book of wonders.

GABRIEL: Good God, is that your business too?

ROSE: It isn't, auntie, true, but I'd like to answer if I may as no one's ever asked me that! He's my first reader! Well, *nothing* is the answer. It's a brand new book of wonders.

GABRIEL: You have your answer, fellow, now go.

HYDE stares at ROSE, then suddenly goes

ROSE: I'd begin the book with him, as he is quite noteworthy, but no one would keep reading and I will one day need readers.

GABRIEL: Put him out of your mind, I dearly hope to.

ROSE: Who is he?

GABRIEL: Nobody on earth,

ROSE: He's the man who brings the letters.

GABRIEL: Damnable… I took a loathing to him at first sight. Even before he behaved so – ugh. the moment I set eyes on him. That's really not like me at all.

ROSE: It's not, is it? And how can one loathe a man who brings you letters?

GABRIEL: I – do not know that, Rose.

ROSE: *I do not like thee, Dr Fell,*
The reason why, I cannot tell,
You can't like everyone, auntie.

GABRIEL: No.

ROSE: I do, but I know I can't. I didn't like him much, but he did show an interest, and not everybody does do.

GABRIEL: *But this I know, and know full well,*

BOTH: *I do not like thee Dr Fell!*

ROSE: So: someone needs a doctor. See *I* don't forget things as quickly as you do!

GABRIEL: Not quickly enough. (The devil take him, he went down my spine like ice.)

ROSE: I say. Is the doctor a friend of yours, Aunt Gabriel?

GABRIEL: Of course not, why would you think so.

ROSE: Because you keep making roses of him.

i.e. GABRIEL keeps crumpling and uncrumpling the letter

GABRIEL: I – well. The doctor was an acquaintance.

ROSE: Why did you say *delirious*?

13

GABRIEL: Cornered, am I.

ROSE: Fair and square!

GABRIEL: Sit down, Rose.

ROSE: In my customary window seat.

GABRIEL: If only for an end to questions... I did, once, know this man, this gentleman I should say, or so I thought him then. Henry Jekyll.

ROSE: Huh? He's the one you did the experiments with?

GABRIEL: He was once, – how on earth would you know a thing like that?

ROSE: I didn't, quite, though I think I rather do now. Doctor Jackal we used to call him.

GABRIEL: I see. Did my brother disclose my entire life to you, Rosemary?

ROSE: Probably. The hours pass slow in Devonshire.

GABRIEL: Well. So be it... I did suspect it was madness. I begin to fear it's disaster, some disease of the cerebellum.

ROSE: Who is he, what's gone wrong with him?

JEKYLL in the old days

GABRIEL: He's a doctor, a surgeon, and he once was simply that. Oh I first met him years ago, at a dinner at the Society, my late husband Arthur was a member, he introduced us, he had important men in hats to talk to, and wanted me entertained I suppose.

ROSE: Dr Jackal was entertaining?

GABRIEL: He was. He was highly respected, Jekyll, well-liked by his colleagues, he was exact and scrupulous, but along

14

with that he had a sort of slyness, a mad impatience at all obstacles, and *that* was quite intriguing...

JEKYLL: My interest is the soul, the duality of the soul!

GABRIEL: The hour was late, much red wine had been taken,

ROSE: That's a horrible drink, I tried some.

JEKYLL: You may well ask what I *mean* by the duality of the soul,

GABRIEL: I may well, yes indeed – what do you *mean* by the duality of,

JEKYLL: The soul,

GABRIEL: Duality of the soul, Dr Jekyll.

JEKYLL: On the moral side, and in my own person, you understand, I have begun to recognize the thorough and primitive *dual nature of man*. I see that, of the two natures that contend in the field of my consciousness, even if I could rightly be said to be either – it is only because *I am radically both*. Both sides of me – are in dead earnest.

GABRIEL: We are all composed of *elements*, Dr Jekyll.

ROSE: *I* was going to say that.

GABRIEL: Well you weren't there.

ROSE: We're a mixture, aren't we.

JEKYLL: Be so good as to call me Henry, Lady Gabriel,

GABRIEL: We are all a mixture, Henry. As Monsieur Lavoisier said.

ROSE: He did and so says Rosemary Palfrey.

JEKYLL: Indeed, but I speak of the very soul: I speak of the angelic and the beastly, the high and the low, the religious man might say – good and evil.

GABRIEL: So might the religious woman.

JEKYLL: Yes,

GABRIEL: Henry.

JEKYLL: Yes, but from an early date, even before the course of my scientific studies began to suggest the *possibility* of such a miracle, I have, how shall I say,

GABRIEL: I don't know how you'll say, do I,

JEKYLL: Dwelt with pleasure – as a beloved daydream – on the thought of –

GABRIEL: The thought of what?

JEKYLL: The separation of these elements.

GABRIEL: *Separation?*

JEKYLL: Indeed so. You smile.

GABRIEL: Do I, I don't mean to.

ROSE: The – *separation of the soul?*

GABRIEL: It was nonsense, I was young. But he provoked my interest.

ROSE: Wait wait. He meant – separating the good soul from the evil? So, you'd be like what, though – one half an angel and one half – *no.*

GABRIEL: In theory, just that. The ultimate extrapolation of the idea would be both Good and Evil made manifest, corporeal, two creatures,

ROSE: I might give red wine another try,

GABRIEL: But as I came to discover, in each field of study
he chose, whether anatomy, or biology, or chemistry,
he would habitually hurry his way to the far side of that
knowledge, the fence at its furthest reach, so as to cast his
eyes into the mist of the next field and the next, and so on
and on, he was ever ranging into the distance. All alone –
as is the fate of such men. But I was young and keen, I
found him fascinating, and for a while I helped him as I
was able.

ROSE: Helped him how, with money?

GABRIEL: Lord no, he's never had want of that. Want of
wisdom, want of measure. I helped in his research.

ROSE: You mean he taught you.

GABRIEL: Taught me? I largely taught myself. I read, Rose,
and I kept reading. I learned what he had learned.

ROSE: So you were a Member of the Society?

GABRIEL: I was the wife of one.

ROSE: But if you knew what *he* knew, they should have let
you join!

GABRIEL: Oh Devonshire lass.

ROSE: What do you mean?

GABRIEL: See if you can guess why I couldn't be a Member.

ROSE: Hmm. I understand. That's not fair at all. We do have
sophisticated people in the county, you know, I count
myself among them, so you worked with him in his actual
laboratory did you,

GABRIEL: For a time.

ROSE: Oh my, I can just see you, you're frowning with concentration and you never spill a drop!

GABRIEL: I prepared the equipment, the cylinders and vessels, I wrote up his notes, I felt I knew the direction his thinking was taking him. As a child I'd devoured picture-books of science, just like you do,

ROSE: You mean did when I was a child. They have tables and diagrams now, and I read carefully and calmly.

GABRIEL: Well it's all to no avail.

ROSE: What do you mean no avail?

GABRIEL: I mean nothing. It's more than ten years since Henry Jekyll became too – fanciful for me.

ROSE: Fanciful? You call curiosity fanciful?

GABRIEL: He began to go wrong, Rose, wrong in mind. I continued to take an interest in him, for old time's sake, as they say,

ROSE: Did you like him as a person?

GABRIEL: Some fields have no boundaries. In some fields nothing's growing.

ROSE: Then climb in and test the soil!

GABRIEL: Oh Rose. Do you not have a *sight* to see, you're the great sight-seer, no? you can't dwell in this city forever, so gather ye rosebuds while ye may.

ROSE: Rosebuds I can get at home. *This* is the sight I'm seeing, Aunt Gabriel – that your old friend is delirious, the doctor needs a doctor, but my aunt abandons him and just crumples up his letters and goes back to her charity work, which is all very well in its way, but I did tell Jenny Gleaner at school *I know a scientist in London!* And she stupidly said *who is he?* like she would and I said *HE – is not anyone! You and your riddles, Rosie,* she went.

GABRIEL uncrumples the last of the letters, the one with the dream

GABRIEL: What makes you think I'm abandoning him.

ROSE: Huh? You're going to see him?

GABRIEL: Call it, as you say, my charity work.

ROSE: Good, I'm glad, so where does he *live* this Jekyll,

GABRIEL: If you go to the window and crane your neck you can see the front of the house from here. The one before the church. I regret this already. It has a dark red door. Not that the door has opened in months, but that was once his medical practice.

ROSE: He lives just over there?

GABRIEL: I believe so, his name was still on the brass when I last walked by, when was it, months ago,

ROSE: Well I'm sorry, Aunt Gabriel, but I cannot let you do such a thing.

GABRIEL: I beg your pardon?

ROSE: It's three hundred yards away and this is a terribly dangerous city, you see, what with the mobs on the street and the mayhem and murders scheduled for this afternoon, I forbid you to go,

GABRIEL: I see emergency makes you merry, Rose,

ROSE: I forbid you to go without a chaperone,

GABRIEL: Oh for heaven's sake,

ROSE: You will have to find a brave young woman to accompany you. Put a notice in The Times, gather all the

candidates, then sit them down in this chair and interview
them one by one.

GABRIEL: Enough, enough, we shall go together, Rose, you
have worn me down. If I sense he's in need of help that
he will not seek of his own accord, whether medical or –
moral, I shall secure it for him. And that will be an end
of it.

ROSE: But Aunt Gabriel, you live three hundred yards from
there, he was a friend of yours, he sent you all these
letters, you didn't answer one and plus you loathe the man
who brings them – why have you changed your mind?

GABRIEL: *[Looking at the letter.]* Because, in the words of Lord
Byron, Dr Jekyll has *had a dream that was not all a dream...*

2

JEKYLL: Gentlemen, I stand here before you today a proud
man, yet a humble one. This great award that you of the
Royal Society – the – Society of Animate Souls... the
Henry Jekyll Society no no... The Royal Progressive Society
– have bestowed upon me renders me profoundly in your
debt. Profoundly grateful. Grateful. Yet I remain at heart
that same young curious man of medicine who... no...
Gentlemen: many say that my work has unlocked a great
door for humanity, hitherto deemed immovable. That
my work has allowed us to see at last into the mirror of
existence, and face up to our own souls as hitherto only
in dreams...we – no... Some of you have asked – many of
you, indeed from every corner of the Empire, you have
written to me for some information about my origins and
I am only too delighted to oblige... I was born in the year
1847 to a large fortune, endowed besides with excellent

parts, inclined by nature to industry, fond of the respect of the wise – no no, they've heard all this before –

GABRIEL: *I* haven't, do go on.

GABRIEL is listening. JEKYLL was lecturing to imaginary peers

JEKYLL: Oh – oh – you, you, you came!

GABRIEL: Still got the key to your theatre, Dr Jekyll.

JEKYLL: Gabriel you came, you saw my letters – why didn't the servant tell me – praise be!

GABRIEL: The old woman? I asked her not to, wanted to watch you in your habitat. I've been hearing that lately you've been poorly, but then I find you accepting major awards in an empty chamber and I realize all's well, still the same old Henry –

JEKYLL: You came, you came, Gabriel, listen I'm on the brink, I need you – I mean I need what you – did you read about the dream? I dreamed and it happened – it happened the same night, I –

He sees ROSE for the first time

GABRIEL: Now what, are you seeing things?

JEKYLL: I – am I? Tell me, I – I beg you –

GABRIEL: Pull yourself together, sir, you think I'd venture here *alone* – having read all your intemperate ravings at one sitting?

JEKYLL: No – I mean – I did not expect another – but her eyes – they look like your eyes looked all that time ago, it's like I see one soul and two of its birthdays walk arm-in-arm in paradise –

ROSE: A pretty theory, Dr Jekyll, but mine is that we have similar expressions because we're kindred: which one do *you* think more persuasive?

GABRIEL: This is my country niece, Henry, Miss Rosemary Palfrey of Devonshire, late arrived in London and more at home here than a cockney. Her days are spent in lectures, her evenings lecturing me.

JEKYLL: Delighted to meet you, Miss Palfrey.

ROSE: I am honoured, Dr Jackal – Jekyll!

GABRIEL: Your name stumbles before you. Another passionate lady of science, I'm afraid.

JEKYLL: Truly kindred, then. Two Gabriels and I!

ROSE: Dr Jekyll, I am awfully fascinated by your work on the soul.

GABRIEL: *Rose!!!*

JEKYLL: What – what have you *told* Miss Palfrey?

GABRIEL: I have told her nothing, for I understand nothing. I remember your ancient fields of interest, which were of public record, and I hear you had a nightmare, I have little else to go on. You look unwell, you look – *determined*, I would not have the demise of my old friend on my conscience, besides which you're fair ruining this excellent old house.

JEKYLL: I am quite well, Gabriel, but I need to speak to you,

GABRIEL: I know, and I am listening in the dark.

JEKYLL: To speak to you alone.

GABRIEL: My niece can be trusted.

ROSE: Pardon?

JEKYLL: You can see I am quite sane and gentle, I've been working late and early, yes I'm weary, that's certain, but do I seem a threat to humankind, Miss Palfrey? Do I seem to you a danger?

ROSE: Not to others, at least, sir.

JEKYLL: So I ask you, Miss Palfrey, will you bide here, while your aunt and I step into the drawing-room for our private discussion? Is that acceptable to you, Gabriel?

GABRIEL: Sane and gentle, truly. Very well, Henry, I believe you pose no mortal threat, I shall learn more of your recent – endeavours. Rose you will bide here.

ROSE: I beg your pardon, *bide*?

GABRIEL: You will stay here in the lecture theatre while Henry and I discuss his research,

ROSE: Behind closed doors. You really mean that, don't you, with the biding,

GABRIEL: Yes I do, miss chaperone, look a whole auditorium for you to lecture to. Your future lies before you, time will pass in no time.

ROSE: You really think I'll do that. Bide. – They really thought I'd do that. Do their biding. Ha! I don't know what *he* thought, Jenny, I couldn't make him out – I did give Aunt Gabriel one last chance, I said, I looked them in the eye... So, you really expect me to sit here, and bide, and do nothing, go eye-to-eye with that clock over there that's in fact wrong, and *not* explore, and *not* go down that dimly-lit corridor for instance, or *not* up that dusty winding stair, and *not* try to find his legendary laboratory?

GABRIEL: She'll sit in every seat, so she can see from every angle.

JEKYLL: A bright spark, you must be proud.

GABRIEL: Proud of myself for coping. No, she's delightful, she sprouted like a sunflower when my back was turned.

ROSE: But I don't think they were listening.

ROSE goes exploring

ROSE: I love that they thought I'd wait there, it made them a bit like children, little Henry and Gabriella. Well now *they're* biding, and I'm making a pilgrim's progress!

She is soon lost in the corridors

ROSE: The House of Doctor Jackal! It's *Jekyll*, Jenny, *Jekyll*. – Stop. I was here before. How can that be? I was also – not here. This is the same place but that lamp was on the right. Or a different place where the lamp is on the left. Wonderland? Or Looking-Glass? Either way, keep walking.

GABRIEL: Henry, since you seem at least partially sane and gentle, perhaps you can explain to me why you would not walk the three hundred yards to my door, instead of sending me your weight in letters.

JEKYLL: I've been working hard, I – the daylight distracts me, I had so much to set down, I thought you'd come when I first wrote,

GABRIEL: Of course you thought that, men do, I nearly didn't come at all, given the bearing of the – the bearer.

JEKYLL: How? What bearer? The old woman took them to your house.

GABRIEL: That's not how they arrived.

ROSE: Now the lamp's on the right again, but it's a green lamp with a moth, deceased. And the passageway is narrower... Moth, fear not, I shall continue this intrepid exploration in your name, I shall find the legendary North-west Passage...

GABRIEL: He said he was a friend in need. He said you sent him.

JEKYLL: He – what did he look like.

GABRIEL: He looked like how he was: blank, lost, an immovable object. One who'd never heard of anything, least of all how human beings behave indoors.

JEKYLL: I see.

GABRIEL: One of your ghouls, is he, one of your resurrectionists? I thought you'd left that line of business behind you.

JEKYLL: I – I have, in as much as I – I need them not – but they hang around on the streets for work, only at night, away from the lamps, I never see their faces, it must have been – it might have been Dobbs, or McFall, perhaps he's – heard of me, he must have taken the letters from the woman, to curry favour with me in some way, perhaps he, I don't know,

GABRIEL: Wants something *from* you, Henry.

JEKYLL: I'll tell the woman not to use him, I'll get rid of him, easily done,

GABRIEL: You know I never saw a man I so disliked – but I can scarce say why. It's not his fault nobody taught him manners,

JEKYLL: You won't see him again.

GABRIEL: I wouldn't know him again, he's just – impossible to describe, yet I declare I can see him at this moment. Explain me that, doctor.

JEKYLL: Forget him, Gabriel, please,

GABRIEL: Oh completely forgotten! So, many thanks for that.

JEKYLL: What matters is where I am, where I've reached,
what it is I'm reaching for,

GABRIEL: Oh is *that* all that matters, like I said, the same old
Henry,

JEKYLL: What I foresaw – what we foresaw – is in reach,
if we only get back to work, you and I together, there's
a missing piece, an element that's lacking in the
compound – and you always had the wit to notice what I
overlooked –

GABRIEL: I notice you're half out of your mind, you're
overlooking that.

ROSE: Jenny Gleaner, I hope you're reading this. If you
are it means I came through alive, though I haven't yet,
so it's not written, I'm just setting it down so it's there
waiting. Dear Jenny, I did not at any time feel afraid in the
corridors of the house of Dr Jekyll. I cheered myself up by
pretending it was all in the past and I was writing a cheery
letter to you in your cottage, which is precisely what I am
doing now – except: I'm not doing it now... oh no this is
all too labyrinthian. Like your house, Dr Henry Jackal.

She lights a match

JEKYLL: You read my letter of the dream.

GABRIEL: I did.

JEKYLL: Explain me that, the matches on my person. The dirt
on my clothes.

GABRIEL: Your house it lit by candles. You don't change and
you don't wash. Was it for this I was begged here with
such unconscionable fervour?

JEKYLL: They were not my brand of matches. The dirt was from the streets. I have not left this house in months.

GABRIEL: What a very impressive witness you'll make on the stand.

JEKYLL: Oh so you think I did it.

GABRIEL: I was joking,

JEKYLL: That I beat that poor girl almost to death?

GABRIEL: I didn't say that. I think you heard about the attack from the cry of a newsboy, then you dreamed about it, and in your exhaustion confounded the dates and think the dream came prior to the event.

JEKYLL: It's not just – that I dreamt it.

GABRIEL: I beg your pardon?

JEKYLL: Say you're right and I did only dream it,

GABRIEL: Of course you only dreamt it – the alternative is impossible,

JEKYLL: Is it really? Am I speaking to Gabriel Utterson or the elders of the church?

GABRIEL: Sarcasm, already?

JEKYLL: When I believed I was doing the deed I described, unaware it was a dream, the cruel assault upon the matchgirl, if indeed it was a dream,

GABRIEL: Yes, what?

JEKYLL: I liked it. I relished it. I loved it.

ROSE: A red lamp, three moths. Well you beat the other fellow but you came to the same conclusion… *How to Escape a Labyrinth*, by Rosemary Palfrey. One: When you reach a junction, don't do what you *would* do. Do what you would *not* do. Hmm. But now, doing what you would *not* do is doing what you *would* do. Start again. One: When you reach a junction, *do* do what you would do. Then suddenly don't do it? Before your mind knows you've changed your mind? No. Think... Got it. One: I'm not afraid. Jenny *would* be afraid, wouldn't you Jenny, so we're opposites in that. So do what *Jenny Gleaner* would do. Run.

She turns, runs, and immediately Jekyll's laboratory moves into place about her. She looks around in awe

JEKYLL: I was a man who was doing it gladly.

GABRIEL: Henry, I am glad you are more or less yourself, and have travelled far along the road I once saw you setting out on – but I shall take my leave directly.

JEKYLL: Let me tell you – I beg you – don't judge me yet –

GABRIEL: I have heard enough,

JEKYLL: You've heard nothing –

GABRIEL: Well nothing's quite enough,

JEKYLL: It's not enough for me! You had a belief, you once held a faith!

GABRIEL: I believed in fairies too but I've not gone looking for them lately.

JEKYLL: Look for this with me – it changes everything we know about our souls!

GABRIEL: It's a poisonous delusion and it's harming your mind,

28

JEKYLL: If the compound is harmful, it's within your capacity to perfect it, Gabriel, there was no one like you, you always had that instinct –

GABRIEL: I've other instincts now. I shall listen. You shall tell me what has happened to you. You shall tell me what you think you need and I shall tell you what *I* think you need. And you shall listen to me.

ROSE has found Jekyll's Notebook

ROSE: Now here's a book of wonders… *A single crystalline salt of white colour… phial half full: blood-red liquor. Highly pungent to sense of smell. Poss* – possibly? – *containing Phos* – phosphorus – *and K* – K? is potassium – *some volatile ether…* then he keeps slightly changing it… *oxidized… aetherized…* different temperatures every time…

ROSE turning the pages

GABRIEL: You drank the thing you made.

ROSE: *First Voyage* – voyage? Voyage. *Pains, grinding…*

JEKYLL: I drank off the compound. Yes, yes… the most racking pains followed – a grinding in the bones, deadly nausea –

ROSE: *Nausea, horror…*

JEKYLL: And a horror of the spirit that, surely, cannot be exceeded at the hour of birth or death –

ROSE: *Presently fading, e.g. after illness…*

JEKYLL: Then these agonies began to subside, and I came to myself as if – out of a great malady – there was something strange in my sensations, something indescribably new – and – from its very novelty – incredibly sweet…

GABRIEL: And beyond that, what?

JEKYLL: Then I found myself in a dream, but so vivid
– *dream* is not the word. It's always the same, I am
walking, running, *hurtling* through the midnight streets
by lamplight, and what I wish to do – is done. Done to –
whomsoever stands in my way. This last dream, with the
girl, this was – simply the most real. She was – standing
in my way. I wanted the – space she took from me – it
belonged to me, I took it, left her screaming on the
ground. Does that sound like me? Does that strike you
like me?

*ROSE is looking through the laboratory, checking bottles and vessels
against what's in the Notebook*

GABRIEL: This is lunacy,

JEKYLL: In the dream I feel – lighter, younger, happier in
my body. There comes a kind of – recklessness, and
then there flows a current of – sensual sights and sounds
– it's like a mill race in my fancy – and I feel the bonds
of obligation, conscience, law, morality – beginning to
dissolve –

ROSE: *5th Oct, nothing, 7th Oct vivid. 11th Oct – triple – total
failure, sleep. 18th Oct, dream no voice. 19th Oct, voice of Not I –
Not I? – then gone, dream, vivid.*

GABRIEL: For the love of God, Henry, we are anything in
dreams,

JEKYLL: But I feel the night wind on my face, I see the chains
of lamps, I can smell the malodours of the river on the air,

GABRIEL: All senses can be dreamed. So all the bonds that
keep you good, all that makes you reasonable, virtuous,
law-abiding, all of these dissolve,

JEKYLL: Even the words for them dissolve…

GABRIEL: Leaving what? What's left when those are gone?

ROSE: *26th Oct voice of I but not I* – I but not I…*2 Nove, girl, vivid*. Girl. Girl. That's the last one. *Compound – 19-V.* After that – a child's scribble… *SHE KNOWS. GET IT. GODS SAKE* (No apostrophe.) *GET ME SOME OF THE OLD.*

JEKYLL: A – freedom. An unknown, never-known, freedom of the soul. In the dream I can do *anything.*

GABRIEL: Henry, enough,

JEKYLL: I feel braced and delighted as if I'd drunk some heavenly spirit –

GABRIEL: Heavenly dreams of violence? I am listening to you – are *you?*

JEKYLL: There were matches in my clothes.

GABRIEL: I don't believe you capable of such a hideous action. I believe the incident happened the night before you dreamed it, and it played on your mind and this – this hellish compound, that exacerbates your sense of reality in sleep – fabricated this illusion.

JEKYLL: Or –

GABRIEL: Or nothing,

JEKYLL: Or – something is – separating from me – I hear a voice, at the edge of a dream I hear a voice that is not my voice – I am not one but two, *I am not one but two!*

ROSE finds the vessel

GABRIEL: God save me I cannot support this work, I shall find you the help you need, but I refuse to contribute to this, this work of –

JEKYLL: Work of whom, the Devil? Behold! My young companion who once upon a time stood in the house she stands in now, infinitely curious at the mysteries of life, her

soul wide open to the starlight, behold her now in early
dotage, babbling of the Devil's work!

GABRIEL: Henry, cease these explorations,

JEKYLL: Cease Galileo, Newton desist, an apple falling is an
apple falling, we have come to the end of knowledge,
close the iron doors of ignorance, there is no more left to
know on earth!

GABRIEL: I shall find you the help you need, my friend, but
communication ends as of this hour,

JEKYLL: No no it *can't*,

GABRIEL: Stand back from me, sir, I'm not a crewman in
your dream,

JEKYLL: Please, Gabriel, I need your knowledge, your
precision, I can't turn back from here in the dark!

GABRIEL: Then turn out of the dark, Henry, come back into
the sunlight,

JEKYLL: The truth lies up ahead, I shall brave the dark to
reach it,

GABRIEL: Or there's nothing there but dark, and it's darkness
draws you on,

JEKYLL: The man I dream is not myself! I am Other, please
God, if I am Other I must know him, I must find him, I
cannot stop now, what becomes of him?

GABRIEL: Becomes of *him*, becomes of *who*? If you need my
– expertise to help you sink further into this – quicksand
then it is in my power to stop you, and I shall assume that
power. I lift you out, I lift you clear. This – compound you
have made, it gives you visions of licence, of depravity,
deviancy, that's all. I believe you dreamed that monstrous
assault on the girl, I believe the time was confused, your

32

work has bewildered you but look at you Henry *look* –
your eyes, your demeanour, you, you speak of separation
– you are separating from your own nature, your reason!
You ventured, you explored, you hoped to – *pioneer*, you
sailed to the world's edge but it doesn't have an edge, and
you find your ship is sailing home again, so be it! your
theory was a theory, there's no shame in having made
one, now please, for the love of God, draw back with
humility, Henry, stand down with grace.

JEKYLL: The Lady has spoken, God save Man from the
Devil's work.

GABRIEL: The Lady speaks it from the heart. – Rose!

JEKYLL: Come trotting home to ignorance,

GABRIEL: Home to what is proven. Rosemary? Rosie? where
is she...

JEKYLL: Gone home to what is proven. Like you.

GABRIEL: In fact cleverer than me. She's found her way out.
So be it. Country manners. Goodbye, Henry.

JEKYLL: I can't let you just walk out –

GABRIEL: You can't *let* me? Can you hear yourself?

JEKYLL: I don't mean that, I mean without you I am utterly –

GABRIEL: Free to begin afresh,

JEKYLL: With what? I am begging you, Lady Gabriel –

GABRIEL: Please do not do that. Please remember who you
are.

*GABRIEL goes. ROSE has placed the compound before her and is
circling it*

33

ROSE: *I do not like thee, Dr Fell*
The reason why, I cannot tell…

JEKYLL distraught he has failed to enlist Gabriel, starting to crack

JEKYLL: Remember who you are, very good, very good, and
who am I indeed, oh gentlemen assembled, I was born
in the year 1847 for no purpose at all, endowed with,
inclined by, fond of, partial to, and I imagined nothing,
found nothing, thought nothing, and I died in the year
what-have-you, sweet dreams and fare thee well.

ROSE approaches the vessel. The 'Dr Fell' rhythm leads her to Blake

ROSE: *Every night and every morn*
Some to misery are born
Every morn and every night
Some are born to sweet delight
Some are born to sweet delight
Some are born to endless night

*ROSE lifts the vessel to her mouth, sniffs it. Then breathes out and
it entirely changes colour. JEKYLL ranting in his fury*

JEKYLL: Ladies and gentlemen, ladies and gentlemen, come
to the Royal Retrograde Society and listen to the world's
last man of science, watch him in his cage, don't feed him,
don't indulge him!

ROSE: Oh, dear God, dear Jenny, dear Jenny, be my witness,
in this letter I write to you now I was safe and sound
again, in the daylight, with the river going by, I didn't
touch the liquid and it, it, it turned some hue I've never
seen, is it my fault if it's sensitive?

JEKYLL begins on his way back to the laboratory

JEKYLL: Ladies and Gentlemen of the Royal Council of
Futility, I am here to reveal the most extraordinary
discovery in the history of humankind. Well may you

stare at me in silence. Is it a new species? Is it an elixir of
immortal life? Can a man fly, can a woman vanish, can a
beast sit down to discuss the economy? NO!

*ROSE hears this cry far off. Terrified, looks for a place to hide the
discoloured compound, finds one, and then a place to hide herself.
She hides just in time, as JEKYLL nears*

JEKYLL: NO! It is that – I have just discovered – that there
is... *nothing left*. Nothing left to discover, nothing left to
know. The Babylonian finger moving on the wall spells
out *THIS IS A WALL*. Turn back, all you miracles and
marvels who had crept to the very edge of our ring of
light, in the hope you would catch our eye. Turn back
into oblivion, into the trees and the deep forests with you
forever, we do not want to know you. We have reached
the very end. The end of revelation.

*JEKYLL begins to make more of the old compound, he doesn't see
ROSE*

JEKYLL: We have reached where there is no more, for all
has been discovered. The Lady of Grace has drawn her
curtain on it all and there is nothing to be shown, nothing
to be learned. Do I hear you cry that Dr Henry Jekyll
isolated a compound that allowed him to approach the
very gate of his own soul? That he could hear the voice
that was *both I and yet not I?* That he needed only to perfect
the compound for the gate to slowly open, for the first
man on earth to meet his own soul in person, ah! but lo,
the Lady of Holy Charity said no, there is nothing left to
know. Put out the fire, stand down with grace, abide in
shadow always.

He raises the compound to his lips

JEKYLL: In the absence of new light: new darkness, more
darkness, more darkness than I ever dared.

He drinks

JEKYLL: Oh it can end me if it likes, I've no means to travel
further. I want it to end me. My desire is that it end me. I
was drowning and the lady sang her song to me, so that I
drowned with grace.

He sways and stares, life a dream to him again

JEKYLL: Come now, conclude, conclude, I do not wish to
remain awake in the world when the revelations end. If I
am denied my meeting with the soul. I am begging you
conclude this, for begging is my trade.

*He falls to his knees, dizzy with the effect of the drug. ROSE sees her
chance to creep away, and she nearly makes it*

JEKYLL: *You.*

ROSE: Dr Jekyll.

JEKYLL: Where are you going.

ROSE: I am going my way, Dr Jekyll.

JEKYLL: Stay.

ROSE: I am afraid. I am not afraid. Jenny would be. Jenny
Gleaner.

JEKYLL: You were here before. You were in the book...

ROSE: I – was lost – and I found myself in here. By a
labyrinthian accident, as it happens. Shall I get you a
doctor doctor – sorry, that sounds, I mean – you have
taken a draught of something, the thing you've been
working on, I find that interesting, so, hmm, what does it
do, what can you see in your experiment may I ask?

JEKYLL: I have taken more than ever...

ROSE: Then perhaps, I should watch what happens?

JEKYLL: You are always here, you're the Angel in the book...

ROSE: I – yes – I am always here, I, I assist you, I prepare the equipment, the cylinders and vessels, so that means, that means you can tell me frankly anything you like,

JEKYLL: You were here long ago, I know your eyes,

ROSE: They're my best feature, some say in the village,

JEKYLL: When did you die, my friend?

ROSE: No, in time I left the village, I didn't die at all, I lived,

JEKYLL: We all die.

ROSE: Look at me. Doctor. Truly.

JEKYLL: An angel then.

ROSE: You – think you're dreaming, don't you. You can tell me anything, you know, I'm very interested in your research on the topic of the Separated Soul among other things – look, look, I'll write your findings down if you like, in your book I found, I didn't *mean* to find it's more like it found *me*,

JEKYLL: I am walking the corridors...

ROSE: Yes, well, so was I, it took a fair while, there should be signposts! maybe, even angels get lost, look I'm writing this down –

JEKYLL: I don't know my way...

ROSE: *You* don't know your way, you live here! what blessed hope did *I* have? I'm writing that neatly, not like the terrible dolt who keeps scribbling here in enormous letters, so go on, what else do you see, you don't know your way, then what happens?

JEKYLL: Then – you are standing there...

37

ROSE: I am – what do you mean?

He simply stares at her

ROSE: Are you – are you still with me, doctor? There is something – changing in your eyes. Doctor? I shall – go now, Dr Jekyll, and leave you to your work, and soon visit you again, and meanwhile ask my aunt to – well. I'll show myself out. Somehow.

She hurries away and is instantly lost in the corridors again, passing lamps and doors and paintings. She hears a male cry of agony nearby. She runs on until she comes to a dead stop. In the shadows is a MAN with his back to her. HYDE

ROSE: Sir, excuse me, the doctor, your master, he's not quite well at all.

HYDE: It is – a new day.

ROSE: What's that?

HYDE: My coat and boots.

ROSE: Remember me, with my book of wonders?

HYDE: He is better.

ROSE: (I have a book of wonders.) he is better then, you feel? The doctor?

HYDE: He needs more.

ROSE: Pardon?

HYDE: I am the one who gets him more.

ROSE: I know you are, you help him, I think you should go to him, he's down that passage.

HYDE: He has gone out.

ROSE: Gone out – where?

HYDE blows, like blowing out a candle. Then nothing. ROSE backs away and runs for it. HYDE very slowly starts stamping his feet, one after the other, till he's walking on the spot, quickening, quickening, as if – warming up. Then he does the same sort of thing with his hands, and then moves his head in circles like exercising neck-muscles. Then he's exercising everything

3

HYDE: Gone out where. No one knows. No one knows me in my coat and boots. My coat and boots and stick by my side.

He gathers a heavy cane

HYDE: Who stick by my side. *I* stick by my side.

A new day, a new dark day out. I don't need a light, lights light my way, lights light for me in my coat and boots, lights light for me. For me my way.

What's my way. No one knows. No one said to. No one made me, not the doctor. I make my way, I need more, it's the morning out, new dark morning out, I need more is my way.

I go where I get more. Could be this way, could be that. No one knows, no one said to, no one made me, not the doctor, I make my way, I say *this* way to go where I get more. This way this way roll up roll up. Walking not walking, running not running, no one said to, no one knows, I go flying not flying, coat flying, tail flying, boots walking in air I go flying no one knows! No one stop me ever. There is no one to stop me. If you stop me you are *not*-me.

ROSE and GABRIEL

ROSE: Did he write to you?

GABRIEL: Don't change the subject, did who write to me?

ROSE: Henry, Henry –

GABRIEL: Oh, *Henry* is it now?

ROSE: Dr Jekyll I mean of course –

GABRIEL: I ask you once again where did you spend the lost hours?

ROSE: I said, I walked along Park Lane, and took in the park, and I saw Nelson of course on Nelson Square, and watched the Fleet flowing under Fleet Street,

GABRIEL: Oh the whole world stops for you to be amusing, I will write to George directly, you have too wild a spirit for this dangerous city, I can't protect you if I don't know where you are! Did you look for his laboratory?

ROSE: Gabriel...

GABRIEL: Oh what happened to *auntie.*

ROSE: I grew when you weren't looking. Like a sunflower, they say.

GABRIEL: Not looking? I can't *find* you when I look!

A CLOAKED GENTLEMAN is sitting on a bench

HYDE: Not-me. Sat there all warm and well, he has more when *I* need more. He has more, he's not-me, *I* need more, stick beside me.

Moon. Moon spots him. Moon spotted him, pointed him out. Out out, spot. There's not-me. No good that. Stood there all warm and well with his more, eh not-me, I'm

40

who needs more, not-me, I'm who needs more, stick with me, stick by my side.

THE GENTLEMAN appears to speak to him

HYDE: What you say, not-me. I don't hear, no one made me. I don't know you, no one said to. Moon spotted you you're spotted. Spotted you, not-me.

THE GENTLEMAN continues speaking but we can't hear. It gets darker, the moon is clouding over. HYDE looks up and thinks he did that

HYDE: Yes moon turn around. I said to so you did do. Not-me, not-me. Did you say you made me. Did you say you know me. No one made me in my coat and boots I stick by my side!

HYDE suddenly attacks THE GENTLEMAN, throwing him to the ground and savagely beating him to death, breaking the cane in two as he does

HYDE: Roll up roll up make way for me, make way for me I'm coming! I was born in eighteen-eighteen-eighteen, all I do is all there is! bang crack crackle goes the bones and the small bones, bang crack crackle!

ROSE: Where did I spend the lost hours? Can we not have secrets? Do we not have shadows as we walk beneath the sun? If we do not have shadows, if we do not have shadows then surely we are not there corporately, we are no one, nothing! Can we not have hours we keep to ourselves, can we not have memories none can share?

THE GENTLEMAN lies still. HYDE examines him. The moon comes out

HYDE: Trickle trickle, not-me.

Tell them all, not-me! Moon and bones, you pass it on!
Stand in my way you jump and trickle! Say you know me,
say you made me, you jump and trickle! You'll be like
you were never, ha! Who's next, who's now? Bang crack
crackle! My coat and boots go flying and flying, more!
More! More! Get more. Get more. Go where I get more.
Make the shapes, make the whole words, make so they
believe me.

HYDE washes his hands

HYDE: There. Better now. There there I'm cleaned. I start
again. Start again with me, my friend? No? Got a cold
shoulder? Gone cold. Sad you are, not-you. Folk will cry,
I'll say I knew him well but he sat there, no one made
me. No one knows me. I need more. I know english. I
get warm, I speak in shapes and decorations, I make the
shapes they make so they believe me, I'm the bearer…

I make the shapes: dear lady, a gentleman is killed, and
I do not know where the doctor is gone to. No one made
me, not the doctor. I will not have the doctor now. He has
gone out. Now I will have more where I get more.

GABRIEL: You'll go wandering in London, will you? Look
who's outside.

ROSE sees HYDE outside, standing very still

GABRIEL: Go arm-in-arm with him, will you?

ROSE: No.

GABRIEL: Go upstairs. I don't want him to see you.

ROSE: Why.

GABRIEL: Because I say so. Because doubtless you'd tell him
more than you'd tell me.

ROSE: Not true, but can we not have secrets, auntie –

GABRIEL: What?

ROSE: Do we not have shadows as we –

GABRIEL: Go! Go! Go!

ROSE hurries out, defiantly muttering the speech anyway as she goes. HYDE is at the window. GABRIEL stares back at him

GABRIEL: *I do not like thee, Dr Fell,*
The reason why, I cannot tell,
But this I know, and know full well...

Why does he assume I'll even open the door? The question is, old girl, why *are* you opening the door.

She opens the door. HYDE just stands there

HYDE: Begging your pardon, my lady.

GABRIEL: Well there's a change. I'll not read any letters.

HYDE: I come with no letters.

GABRIEL: What's your business then. Is the doctor still with us?

HYDE: I know not, Lady Gabriel.

GABRIEL: Lady Gabriel is it now, well consider me elevated, where is he.

HYDE: I know not. He went out last night.

GABRIEL: Where?

HYDE: I know not.

GABRIEL: You come here to tell me you know not. So. I am told, good day.

HYDE: New day, a new day.

GABRIEL: Well indeed, and I have much to do therein, so if you wouldn't mind, Mr,

HYDE: Hyde.

GABRIEL: Pardon?

HYDE: A gentleman is murdered.

GABRIEL: I – I see, are you the newsboy now?

HYDE: I am the bearer.

GABRIEL: The bearer of the news, well this is London town at the end of the century, someone's always murdered,

HYDE: Sir Danvers Carew. Read all about it.

GABRIEL: I see.

HYDE: Member of the Parliament slain.

GABRIEL: How dreadful. He was – a friend of Henry's.

HYDE: He is not one now.

GABRIEL: What?

HYDE: He was beaten to death on Castle Street, read all about it.

GABRIEL: On Castle Street – heavens no, when?

HYDE: Last night.

GABRIEL: Good God.

HYDE: *His* last night.

GABRIEL: Spare me your gallows wit – you say the doctor was out?

HYDE: I know not where.

GABRIEL: But that's – that's impossible.

HYDE: What is.

GABRIEL: It is not your place to ask me that.

HYDE: Where is the book of wonders.

GABRIEL: I beg your pardon?

HYDE: The girl with the book of wonders.

GABRIEL: She – it's none of your business, gone, gone, on a train somewhere like she never came,

HYDE: I heard her speaking to you.

GABRIEL: I – good God are you calling me a liar?

HYDE: I heard her voice and your voice.

GABRIEL: Of course you did, I was missing her, fool, she's on a ship sailing west forever, I missed her so I spoke in her voice, we do that, we are kindred, do you understand?

HYDE: You – spoke in her voice. You made her.

GABRIEL: Please depart.

HYDE: No one made me.

GABRIEL: Be gone, damn you!

HYDE: I need more. It is evening.

GABRIEL: It's the morning, are you ill? Go sleep it off.

HYDE: Help me, I need more.

GABRIEL: What did you say?

HYDE: I am going out.

HYDE, weakening, staggers away. ROSE comes

45

ROSE: I heard what he was asking.

GABRIEL: Yes, and he heard you crying out. The walls of a city are too thin for your kind, Rose, go home to the wattle-and-daub and shriek to your heart's content.

ROSE: This isn't to be shrieked, it's to be whispered gravely.

GABRIEL: Oh? Is that because for once it isn't just a story?

ROSE: Yes. I am sorry. Aunt. I have a confession to make.

GABRIEL: Do you now.

ROSE: I did go to Henry's laboratory.

GABRIEL: Of course you did, you and old Henry,

ROSE: There. That's that said. I got lost in his house, that's all.

GABRIEL: Got lost how, I said stay in the lecture-room.

ROSE: You said *bide*, I didn't know that word.

GABRIEL: That's eyewash, girl.

ROSE: I was frightened, that was true, it was dark in there, do you even *know* about his house, it goes on and on forever, you were once his assistant!

GABRIEL: Long ago and the lab was on the Street side.

ROSE: Well it isn't now, it's through the lecture-theatre, then along a lot of narrow passageways then out across a courtyard, then up a winding stair, and through some sort of abattoir and more doors, more corridors,

GABRIEL: Ooh, no one gets lost like Rose gets lost,

ROSE: But I didn't see your doctor, and I didn't touch his work things, I left it all quite undisturbed,

GABRIEL: The trouble with storytellers is,

ROSE: I'm telling the truth now, Gabriel!

GABRIEL: You don't ask them for directions.

ROSE: What do you mean? I didn't touch a thing! Do you know what's at the furthest end?

GABRIEL: Oh, at a pinch, Death?

ROSE: I fled the place, I was afraid, I found a door and it gave out on the street, it was a black door, stained and blistered, a door I saw the day I came to London, it scared me for some reason, as if I knew what lay ahead, I remember wondering what was behind it,

GABRIEL: Well now you know: *you are.*

ROSE: It's on Castle Street, his back door lies on Castle Street, where that murder was.

GABRIEL: And Henry dreamed he did it, doubtless, and woke up with the old man's blood on his hands,

ROSE: What if Henry's right?

GABRIEL: *Henry Henry Henry –*

ROSE: What if the thing he said could be done – *can be done!*

GABRIEL: Pack your things.

ROSE: Or *has been done?*

GABRIEL: You're booked on the Great Western,

ROSE: The separation of souls!

GABRIEL: You're going home tomorrow.

ROSE: I am home.

GABRIEL: I am saying you have to leave.

ROSE: Why would I leave I'm home.

47

GABRIEL: Oh for goodness sake Rose –

ROSE: Not *your* home, Gabriel, London Town.

GABRIEL: You have no house in London!

ROSE: Nor do half the Londoners, as far as I can see.

GABRIEL: You are booked on the Great Western, I'll hear no
more,

ROSE: Oh I'm a bad hand at lying. I want to put things
straight before we part.

GABRIEL: I don't want us to part, it's for your safety, heaven
knows, I did try to make this clear before you even set
foot in here –

ROSE: I did find the laboratory!

GABRIEL: So you said.

ROSE: And I did meet Jekyll there!

JEKYLL waking in his laboratory, finding the broken cane

GABRIEL: I see.

ROSE: I was frightened all alone in that grand empty theatre,

GABRIEL: So you did the sensible thing and ran around a
pitch-dark building of which you knew nothing,

ROSE: I was lost I grant, and then I happened on his
workplace, and I did nothing there, except I did look at
his notebook, there's much to say about that, you know, it
has your handwriting very near the start, and near the end
it has some terrible scribble of infantile things in capital
letters,

GABRIEL: What else did you do.

JEKYLL writing in his Notebook

JEKYLL: I know this cannot reach you, Angel-of-the-Book, but your presence in my mind gives me strength. I dreamed of what he did, the Other, the One I am not. I dreamed it, but – by God I can turn from it no more – what was only dream to me – was enacted by that Other. By that Other, into whose mentality I have helplessly spiralled, I know not how or why. I had spoken of him to my one-time friend, the Lady who would shut the gates on all question, and I believe that for this reason that Other, who had long been caged, came out roaring, in a fury –

ROSE: Nothing, it was an accident, and it only changed the colour a little,

GABRIEL: What did you do.

ROSE: I – sniffed a transparent compound, called 19-V, which was mentioned in the notebook, it was significant and it slightly changed in colour.

GABRIEL: To what.

ROSE: To – not quite as clear as it was.

GABRIEL: To what.

ROSE: To a pale, slightly deeper, slightly darker – purple.

GABRIEL: Purple. Darker than clear then.

ROSE: Yes, to be precise, a bit darker than clear.

GABRIEL: Ha well I'm he sure won't notice that.

ROSE: He might, the point is, don't you see, it is I, Rosemary Palfrey, who has tainted his compound and maybe directly threatened his wellbeing!

GABRIEL: Only Henry Jekyll has threatened his wellbeing.

ROSE: Still. I've spoiled his work.

GABRIEL: Does he know you did that?

JEKYLL: I felt a tempest of impatience, I saw the old man sitting there, in a dream, I still believed! I listened to his helpless civilities – no sane man could have struck on such a pitiful provocation – and when I struck – the Other struck, not I!

ROSE: I hid it, I was embarrassed, I must have breathed upon it, that's an elementary error so I hid myself,

GABRIEL: Let me guess, in a sort of lamp, like a genie,

ROSE: An elementary error, and I only emerged because he seemed in such despair I couldn't help it!

GABRIEL: In despair. Why.

ROSE: I think because you wouldn't help him. But you can now, don't you see? We can go together, and I can speak of my accidental error, and we can help him make the chemical he needs, and he won't die, and then maybe –

GABRIEL: You, Rose, are getting on the Exeter train in the morning, and I – well, you have no need of knowing what I'll do, you'll be gone won't you.

ROSE: Why won't you help him? Are you angry that I want to?

GABRIEL: I'm not angry at all. I just know what's right and wrong.

ROSE: That's it? That's all? Does you knowing what's right and wrong mean you just stop feeling what happens to human creatures?

GABRIEL: You don't know what I feel. You only know what *you* feel, and you base all life upon it.

ROSE: Right. So I'll go. Good morning cows, good evening
apple orchard, good morrow what, knitting a sock,
but won't you at least tell him what happened to his
compound?

GABRIEL: If you leave tomorrow. If you leave tomorrow I'll
tell him.

JEKYLL starts writing in his Notebook

ROSE: Then I will leave tomorrow. *Then I will leave tomorrow*, I
told her, but I haven't done that, Jenny, I have packed my
things but left them there without me in my room...

JEKYLL: I will not delay too long to bring all writing to an
end. The Other will smear his filth across it, if he does
not tear it to pieces in his ape-ish spite. The doom that
is closing on us both has already changed and crushed
him...

ROSE: I left the house on The Regent's Street, no time to
speak to him today, *what's wrong today, Rose?* he goes,
Nothing, I say, I have gone wandering through London in
the clothes of one that none would look upon. It is a thing
I love to do...

JEKYLL: He does not want to die. He would like the lamp to
burn through the night. One final time I cast my mind
around every space in this chamber, from the dustiest
shelf to the narrowest cranny. I cannot find the compound.
The miracle is finished. There is no more by which I can
make what makes me alive. It is gone from existence and
I can by no means venture out to gather what I need. The
forces of morality are circling me like crows.

ROSE: I have taken nothing with me but some apples from
the crystal bowl, an extra shawl for the nights that get so
chilly, and the key to an old black door that backs onto
Castle Street. These are the last things I shall borrow,

Jenny Gleaner, and knowing you you shall hold me to it. Yours always, Rose. PS. Alas. I forgot my book of wonders.

ROSE heads out into the streets, JEKYLL has unlocked a drawer and brought out a phial of a milk-white substance he prepares to drink

JEKYLL: This is the true hour of my death, and what follows will concern another than myself. Here then, as I lay down the pen, and proceed to seal up my confession, I bring the life of that unhappy Henry Jekyll to –

Something is dawning on him. There's a place he hasn't looked. He looks, and find the vessel of liquid Rose breathed upon. He sniffs it, tastes it

JEKYLL: The same, the same as the old! The same in everything but colour! Dark sister to my clear life! The angel's finger pointed to this place!

He begins to drink

JEKYLL: It's the same, the same – but hold, not all… keep some back, have I the strength to keep some back? Yes, I shall, I do, keep, keep… I do have some – blessed strength left…

He puts the rest of it back where it was. This compound is stronger than before

JEKYLL: Oh life, life *at* me, life *in* me, life *through* me!

He staggers back to his Notebook to write in it

JEKYLL: As it was, as it was, as it was the first time, the same as the old but coursing through me, oh…

It works on him, he drops the pen, staggers

JEKYLL: I see, I see, I – see.

JEKYLL sees HYDE standing there. They have never seen each other

JEKYLL: Are you there? – Who are you? – Where have you come from?

HYDE: It is – a new day.

JEKYLL: Yes, a new day, come, come, I waited – I – why are you, why are you not as I?

HYDE: Why are you not as I.

JEKYLL: Do you know me?

HYDE: Do you know me.

JEKYLL: I know I have – reached you.

HYDE: Reached me.

JEKYLL: Raised you up, I led you here into the light,

HYDE: You, why are you not as I. Where am I.

JEKYLL: Where, here, with me,

HYDE: I like – to be here.

JEKYLL: I too, we are – together,

HYDE: It is a new day. It was so dark.

JEKYLL: I am weakening, I cannot stay,

HYDE: Stay, it was so dark.

JEKYLL: I need to ask you,

HYDE: Stay,

JEKYLL: I shall stay, share my lantern-light,

HYDE: Lantern-light,

JEKYLL: Shelter, be at peace now,

HYDE: I was alone, and now,

JEKYLL: I am with you,

HYDE: I am with you. Who.

JEKYLL: I. And I ask, as I must, why do you do – what things
    you do?

HYDE: It is a new day, I am free. I do what things.

JEKYLL: You do them. Why.

HYDE: I have not known – why not to.
    Who wakes me, who says to,
    who makes me want and wish, who makes my way
    before me makes the smile to smile within me
    and light the world so I don't see for light!
    Who makes my coat and boots to go so brightly
    and has me step my step like I am watched for
    for I would have my name in the book of wonders
    and not be, not be turned
    with pages to the dark. I was in the dark.
    I want the light now, and no dark again,

JEKYLL: Be at peace, do no harm,

HYDE: I want the light, I will be free, not dark again, no dark
    again,

JEKYLL: Do no harm I beg you, do no wrong, hurt no soul
    out there!

HYDE: Who are you.

JEKYLL: I?

HYDE: You are not I.

JEKYLL: It is my light you come by,

HYDE: *My* light *my* light,

JEKYLL: Stay by my light,

HYDE: Go out.

HYDE blows the light out

JEKYLL: No stay with me!

HYDE: Who, why,

JEKYLL: I am fading,

HYDE: You are fading, why,

JEKYLL: I cannot stay,

HYDE: Go out then. The dark again for you now.

JEKYLL: Do no wrong I beg you...

HYDE: Who. Why not to.

JEKYLL: I am the light, stay with me...

HYDE: Who are you who went out.

JEKYLL: Or I shall end it...

HYDE: End what.

JEKYLL: End us, I shall end us...

HYDE: End what.

JEKYLL fades and is gone

HYDE: Ended. Who were you. Not I. Gone out. End us shall you? You are not us. You are ended, I stay. I am the light now. Do no wrong I beg you. Who are you to. No one made me. A new day. A cold sky for me only. What am I for if not what I want.

HYDE goes to the book and scrawls across it, spits on it, abuses it

HYDE: End it shall you he he he, you are ended not me. She
knows. Get her. Godsake. Can we not have secrets auntie.

HYDE growing to greater force than before, exercising

HYDE: Can we not have secrets auntie do we not have
shadows. I forgot my book of wonders. I wander winding
streets as I had faces. I had no blank page and nowhere I
forgot my book of wonders. She knows. Godsake get her.
Good morning. Top of the morning.

4

Dark outside. GABRIEL is reading Rose's book of wonders

GABRIEL: *The Lost Hours, by R. G. Palfrey...* Little trickster,
where in heaven have you vanished to...

ROSE creeps into the laboratory

ROSE: Dr Jekyll? Dr Jekyll? Henry?

She looks at the Notebook

ROSE: This was Henry lately, look it's barely dry – *Searched
a last time. Eureka* (Ancient Greek, meaning I've found it.)
*Eureka, same as was, but colour v, unknown before, call Zero-V.
Last time. Will end this.* Will end this... Then this – gigantic
– baby script: *GON GON GON. ENDED YOU. NO ONE
MADE ME.* No one made me...

*ROSE takes the Notebook and hurries out. Back in the house
GABRIEL reads on. A knock on the door. ROSE's voice*

ROSE: Auntie! Auntie!

GABRIEL: Oh thank God, thank God!

ROSE: I forgot my book of wonders! I forgot my book of wonders!

GABRIEL: I have it, I'm reading it, and I won't let you leave!

GABRIEL throws open the door. It isn't Rose it's HYDE. In his own voice now

HYDE: Can we not have secrets auntie.

She freezes, he comes in

HYDE: Will you be wise. Will you be guided.

GABRIEL: Wh-what –

HYDE: Will you suffer to go forth.

GABRIEL: I – what –

HYDE: You need to make it.

GABRIEL: Make what – you mean for Jekyll? –

HYDE: Who, no, make it for me. I won't have the dark again. I am the light, come with me.

GABRIEL: I'm not going anywhere.

HYDE: I saw the candlelight it's lighting everything around it.

GABRIEL: What –

HYDE: Everything is light. I see it is London in the light, man and ladies arm in arm, off we trot.

GABRIEL: I will not go with you,

HYDE: I want this, I am free, you need to make it so I stay.

By force he takes her by the arm and they walk out into the London streets

HYDE: Man and ladies arm in arm.

GABRIEL: Someone, someone help – I do not want to be walking with this person! Excuse me, sir, madam?

HYDE: I know London in the light and dark, nobody is listening.

GABRIEL: Can you help me please? they can see it in my eyes, these are my neighbours,

HYDE: What are neighbours.

GABRIEL: My friends,

HYDE: They looked away look, they want to see the man and ladies arm in arm, good morning to ye ma'am, sir, ma'am, sir, ma'am it is easy in the light, off we trot.

GABRIEL: Let me go, Hyde, in God's name I can't help you, will someone help me out please, this isn't what it looks like!

HYDE: They like what it looks like, the man and ladies want to see the man and ladies walking.

GABRIEL: Somebody help me please!

HYDE: The fine clothes are looking away and the ragged clothes are laughing now your dark is like their dark.

GABRIEL: To hell with you,

HYDE: Whats hell.

GABRIEL: What have you done to Henry,

HYDE: Whats Henry.

GABRIEL: Where is he? oh God help me –

HYDE: Nobody made me auntie.

GABRIEL: Where are we going, to Henry?

HYDE: Home. Where you will make it.

GABRIEL: Make what, I don't know how he makes it,

HYDE: Make it so I stay.

GABRIEL: I don't want you to stay, who are you?

HYDE: So I stay for all of time.

GABRIEL: What?

HYDE: So I stay in the light for all of time.

They are in the house, in the corridors with the lamps, then the laboratory

GABRIEL: Henry! Henry!

HYDE: He is ended, be at peace.

GABRIEL: Is there a servant in these ruins? Somebody help me!

HYDE: Whats a servant.

GABRIEL: I am Lady Gabriel Utterson, I am here against my will, the name of the man who is holding me is –

HYDE: Alone.

GABRIEL: I can't help you. Have mercy.

HYDE: What's mercy?

GABRIEL: When you do not do – what you could do.

HYDE: I am a free man in the light, it is a new game, I do anything.

GABRIEL: What is it you think I can do?

HYDE: Make it. Make it better for me so I stay in the light for all of time.

GABRIEL: That cannot be done.

HYDE: You do it or you end.

GABRIEL: It cannot be done by anyone on earth.

HYDE: *You* do it.

GABRIEL: I do what.

HYDE: You stay in the light for all of time.

GABRIEL: I – do not. Oh my God poor soul, you are mad. I
will end one day. We all will poor love.

HYDE: I will not. Not I. Make it now, then you will end.

GABRIEL: I am to end if I make it for you and end if I do not?

HYDE: You are in my light and you must end, make it for me
or I will make you into bits of you, bang, crack, crackle.

GABRIEL: I see. Then let me tell you this, if I'm to, as you say,
end with a – well. I *do* know how to make it. I was told
how by my country niece. She's a scientist and I'm proud
of her and *that* goes to the end of time. But I will not
make it for you. I choose not to. I would rather end in the
knowledge that in a matter of hours they will hang you.

HYDE: You do know how to make it.

GABRIEL: I could do it in my sleep.

HYDE: Do it.

GABRIEL: I choose not to.

HYDE: Do it or you end now. That. Or this. That. Or this.

GABRIEL: I do not believe in that or this. That or this is
the language of death. I believe in everything that lives
between.

HYDE: What's between. Nothing lives between. Make it.

GABRIEL: No.

HYDE: Make it. It is evening. I need it.

GABRIEL: What?

HYDE: It is evening, poor coat and boots, make it better.

GABRIEL: I shall not.

HYDE is weakening. He roars in anger and shapes to attack her, she drops to the ground, he stumbles, dizzy, confused

GABRIEL: *Our Father, who art in heaven, hallowed be thy name –*

HYDE: Nobody made me, I made me.

GABRIEL: *Thy kingdom come, thy will be done,*

HYDE: Make me stay for all of time.

GABRIEL: *On earth as it is in heaven,*

HYDE: I would not be, I would not, it is evening, it is evening, stay.

GABRIEL realizes, sees her chance, and runs past him. He flails at her and misses, she flees into the night

HYDE: Stay. In my lantern-light.

JEKYLL is there, HYDE falls

JEKYLL: I am here.

HYDE: It is evening. Light the lantern-light.

JEKYLL: Go now, be at peace,

HYDE: No, not the dark. Not the dark.

JEKYLL: I am here.

HYDE is gone, JEKYLL, weaker than ever, goes to find his Notebook and finds it gone. ROSE has it

ROSE: Are you looking for this, Henry.

JEKYLL: Angel-of-the-book –

ROSE: Miss Rosemary Palfrey.

JEKYLL is pointing to where she hid the vessel, ROSE gets it, half is left

ROSE: Mea culpa (Latin, meaning all my fault.) I didn't mean to do it.

JEKYLL: How – it's the compound – but what did you do, you changed it,

ROSE: I swear I never meant to,

JEKYLL: You made it more – it was stronger, you made me see him, I set eyes on him, we spoke, we shared the light, it brought us into the light together, what did you do, what in God's name did you do?

ROSE: We did nothing, God and I, I mean all I did was…

JEKYLL: Tell me, it changes everything!

ROSE: You know I think I'll hold my horse just now, till I learn a little more. Where I come from, no one taught me anything, so I always had to bargain.

JEKYLL: What?

ROSE: Tell me what you saw and I'll tell you how I made it.

JEKYLL: I cannot.

ROSE: Then I will not. Have you got the strength to write it down?

JEKYLL: No, I am empty, I am done.

ROSE: Then the world will never know what you accomplished. Unless some other person in this room happens to be standing upright with a working ink-pen and a notebook, does that sound like you, Dr Jekyll?

JEKYLL: You will write it all?

ROSE: I will write it all.

JEKYLL: I… I saw him. I saw the face of the Other.

ROSE: In your mind? In a dream?

JEKYLL: In this room. Right where you're standing. I saw myself. The man who brought the letters.

ROSE: Him? He is – part of you?

JEKYLL: You don't believe.

ROSE: Alone in the world I do. He is – he is your soul?

JEKYLL: Myself, and separate from myself. I don't want you to see him.

ROSE: I've seen him twice, I've lived to tell the tale.

JEKYLL: Not now. Before, he was the part of me that needed Gabriel to help make the compound. It would say anything. It didn't hurt her or you. It thought it needed you. Now it knows it has to die.

ROSE: No!

JEKYLL: I am a good man. A just man. I have chosen my course and drawn my conclusion.

ROSE: You can't just – I want to see the proof of it. What you say you saw.

JEKYLL: You cannot mean that.

ROSE: I am a scientist, I mean everything. Drink the rest of it.

63

JEKYLL: I don't want you to see it.

ROSE: I'm not afraid of what I can imagine, sir.

JEKYLL: You can't imagine this.

ROSE: Don't tell *me* what I can't imagine!

The distant sound of voices, a CROWD, police whistles

ROSE: You've drawn a crowd there, doctor, the Royal Society of Shrieking and Smashing,

JEKYLL: All things will end tonight.

ROSE: A shilling says they won't, but if we both catch sight of him and only *I* come back, at least I'll tell it to the world. Drink it.

JEKYLL: We have a bargain. I have told you faithfully what I saw. What did you add to the compound?

ROSE: Oh it's complicated,

JEKYLL: Not to me!

ROSE: It's so complicated we'll probably have to say when the work is published: *The Incredible Discovery Of Dr H. Jekyll and Miss R. G. Palfrey On the Subject Of the Duality Of the Soul.*

JEKYLL: It's my life's work, Miss Palfrey,

ROSE: It's mine too, it's just a shorter life so far, but you do come first in the alphabet, true,

JEKYLL: You'll be cited in the Appendix,

ROSE: The what? oh that passed right over my head, I better go and find a husband and ask him what Appendix means.

JEKYLL: Of course, of course, granted, you have helped me,

64

ROSE: If we could shake on that contract, please, thank you,

JEKYLL: Good God what new race are you part of.

ROSE: The other half of yours. So. Now we are a team. We trust each other, Henry. Drink and I'll tell you what I did.

JEKYLL drinks the vessel dry

JEKYLL: Some kind of ethanol – zinc? a plant essence? an opiate confection? laudanum – or the camphorated tincture?

ROSE: Doctor I breathed on it.

JEKYLL: You did what?

ROSE: I breathed on it. I didn't even sip it, to be honest, I'm not as reckless as they say in the parish. I breathed on the clear liquid and it blushed before my eyes. There was a boy like that at the Maypole dance one time.

JEKYLL: That was it?

ROSE: That was it for him.

JEKYLL: Human cells – addition of distinct nuclei precipitating –

ROSE: Do you have time for this? Your audience is coming. Then again they'll take forever to find this lab of yours. It took *me* long enough and they all sound stupid.

JEKYLL: That's the last of it. What I need – there is no more of.

ROSE: Though we both know how it's made now. How sad. For science I mean.

JEKYLL: I am a good man, a righteous man, do not make what I have made.

ROSE: I am – a woman of science. Sir.

65

JEKYLL: So learn from what I've done. Swear you will turn back.

ROSE: I am a woman of science, I –

JEKYLL: You alone will see what I have done. You will have the book. Tell the story. It is your story now.

ROSE: You have my word.

JEKYLL: When he first comes he is weak. The instant you see him, run, run. That way you live, that way you can honestly write what you saw. But do one thing for me first.

ROSE: Anything, Henry. Most things.

He gropes for a tiny key and gives it to her

JEKYLL: Third from the right, it's always locked.

ROSE: I know it is.

JEKYLL: There's a small phial of milk.

ROSE: I see there is. It isn't milk, though, is it, Henry.

JEKYLL: No, it isn't milk.

ROSE: But it's what you drink last thing.

JEKYLL: Yes, Miss R. G. Palfrey, it's what you drink last thing.

ROSE: (It's Rosemary Georgina.)

JEKYLL waning, HYDE appears from the shadows, begun again, bewildered

HYDE: It is a new day.

JEKYLL: Do you see him –

ROSE: I see him –

JEKYLL: Now go, now go –

ROSE: I shall not –

HYDE: Me, my coat and boots.

JEKYLL: Save yourself for God's sake Rose –

ROSE: Hush now, no excitement, let's save that for the book.

HYDE: Oh I would have my name in the book of wonders
and not be turned into the dark.

ROSE: The book is waiting for you, Henry –

JEKYLL: He wants the light – he wants to stay in the light –

ROSE: Henry, Henry – it's you, *you* want to stay in the light –

JEKYLL: Oh – I do –

ROSE: No one made you as you are – you were free, you
were always free and you want to stay in the light –

JEKYLL: Oh I do, Rose, I do –

ROSE: You can share the light, do you see – you want the
same light, the same new day,

JEKYLL: Yes, yes –

ROSE: He is you and you are he, be one now, be at peace,

JEKYLL: Yes, come in, I am with you, I am *for* you, I am here,

ROSE: You did the things you did, Henry, *you, you*, be at one
now, be at peace,

JEKYLL: Come in, my friend, come into the light and be at
peace – come once and stay for always, come once and
stay for always…

HYDE comes to him

JEKYLL: All you did, my friend, *I* did, *I* did, not you but I, I
carry you, I bear you, I am the bearer, let us sail now, it

is evening, let us only sail together, friend, so no soul can part us…

They are bound together and then HYDE is gone within him. JEKYLL looks up at ROSE for the last time

JEKYLL: My new day, my coat and boots, my lantern-light.

He raises the phial to ROSE as if to bid her goodbye, and drinks it. ROSE puts her finger to her lips, ssshhh. She gets away, with the Notebook, before the CROWD arrives. Their noise is tumultuous, they are smashing up everything Slow fade to darkness

* * *